DAILY DEVOTIONS FOR Mothers

DAILY
DEVOTIONS
FOR
Mothers

365
INSPIRATIONAL READINGS

HUMBLECREEK
INSPIRATION FOR LIFE

© 2006 by Barbour Publishing, Inc.

ISBN 1-59789-452-4

Compiled by Joanie Garborg.

Text is taken from *Daily Wisdom for Mothers* by Michelle Medlock Adams, published by Barbour Publishing, Inc. Quotations and prayers may have been edited slightly to allow them to stand alone.

Cover image © PhotoDisc

Scripture quotations marked KJV are taken from the King James Version of the Bible.

All scripture quotations, unless otherwise indicated, are taken from the Holy Bible, New International Version®. NIV®. Copyright © 1973, 1978, 1984 by International Bible Society. Used by permission of Zondervan. All rights reserved.

Scripture quotations marked MSG are taken from THE MESSAGE. Copyright © by Eugene H. Peterson 1993, 1994, 1995, 1996, 2000, 2001, 2002. Used by permission of NavPress Publishing Group.

Scripture quotations marked NASB are taken from the New American Standard Bible, © 1960, 1962, 1963, 1968, 1971, 1972, 1973, 1975, 1977, 1995 by the Lockman Foundation. Used by permission.

Scripture quotations marked CEV are from the Contemporary English Version © 1991, 1992, 1995 by American Bible Society. Used by permission.

Scripture quotations marked NKJV are taken from the New King James Version. Copyright © 1979, 1980, 1982 by Thomas Nelson, Inc. Used by permission. All rights reserved.

Scripture quotations marked TLB are taken from *The Living Bible* copyright © 1971. Used by permission of Tyndale House Publishers, Inc., Wheaton, Illinois 60189. All rights reserved.

Scripture quotations marked NLT are taken from the *Holy Bible,* New Living Translation, copyright © 1996. Used by permission of Tyndale House Publishers, Inc. Wheaton, Illinois 60189, U.S.A. All rights reserved.

Scripture quotations marked AMP are from the Amplified Bible, © 1954, 1958, 1962, 1964, 1965, 1987 by The Lockman Foundation. Used by permission.

Published by Humble Creek, P.O. Box 719, Uhrichsville, Ohio 44683

Printed in the United States of America.
5 4 3 2 1

JANUARY 1

"Come to me, all you who are weary and burdened,
and I will give you rest."
Matthew 11:28

There's not a lot of rest in a mother's schedule. But that's not really the kind of rest this verse is talking about. The rest mentioned in this verse is the kind of rest that only Jesus can provide. Resting in Jesus means feeling secure in Him and allowing His peace to fill your soul. That kind of rest is available to all—even mothers.

JANUARY 2

Cast all your anxiety on him because he cares for you.
1 Peter 5:7

No matter how many challenges you face today, you can smile in the face of aggravation. How? By casting your cares upon the Lord. Yet many of us feel compelled to take all of the cares upon ourselves. We can handle anything that comes our way, right? Wrong! But God can. When the day starts to go south, cast your cares on Him. He wants you to!

JANUARY 3

God is our refuge and strength,
an ever-present help in trouble.
Psalm 46:1

Often after God rescues us, we cling to Him until we're safe. Then we go about our own lives until we need Him again. Wouldn't it be better if we just stayed close to Him all the time—not just in troubled times? Then we wouldn't have to panic. He'd already be there.

JANUARY 4

"Who of you by worrying can
add a single hour to his life?"
Matthew 6:27

God tells us in His Word that worry is a profitless activity. Worrying about our children may feel like a natural thing to do, but in reality it's sin. If we are constantly worrying about our kids, it's like saying to God, "I know that You created the universe, but I'm not sure You know what's best for my children. So, I'll handle them, God."

JANUARY 5

All you need to remember is that
God will never let you down;
he'll never let you be pushed past your limit;
he'll always be there to help you come through it.
1 Corinthians 10:13 MSG

Whether you work outside the home or at home—you're busy. When you feel that overwhelming sense of "I don't think I can do one more thing today" taking over—stop! Breathe deeply and remember that God promised He'd never give you more than you can handle. Isn't that good news?

JANUARY 6

I call on you, O God,
for you will answer me;
give ear to me
and hear my prayer.
Psalm 17:6

Prayer should be instinctive. God should be the first One we "call" in every situation. Make sure He is first on your speed dial.

JANUARY 7

"For I know the plans I have for you,"
declares the LORD,
"plans to prosper you and not to harm you,
plans to give you hope and a future."
Jeremiah 29:11

*G*od has a plan for your children's lives—better than you could ever imagine. So, relax. If you've given your children to God, you've given them the best chance to succeed that you could ever give them!

JANUARY 8

"But seek first his kingdom
and his righteousness,
and all these things
will be given to you as well."
Matthew 6:33

I'm happy to say that there is life after lists. I am a recovering to-do list maker. I've found such freedom in trusting God with my daily activities. Sure, I still have reminder sticky notes scattered around my house, but now I'm not ruled by a list. I've learned there is sweet rest and freedom in trusting God with my day.

JANUARY 9

I can do everything through him
who gives me strength.
Philippians 4:13

God's Word says that we can do all things through Christ who gives us strength. All means all, right? So no matter how you feel today, you can accomplish whatever is on your plate. See, you don't have to feel powerful to be powerful. The God in you is all-powerful, and He will cause you to triumph.

JANUARY 10

"Be still,
and know that I am God."
Psalm 46:10

As moms, we're sometimes afraid to trust God with our children. But, what we fail to realize is this—He loves them even more than we do. He loved them before we ever held them in our arms. We can trust Him with our kids.

JANUARY 11

I will say of the LORD,
"He is my refuge and my fortress,
my God, in whom I trust."
Psalm 91:2

*T*hank You, Lord, for taking care of my children better than I can. Amen.

JANUARY 12

There is a time for everything,
and a season for every
activity under heaven.
Ecclesiastes 3:1

*M*any times in our quest to be the perfect mom, we lose sight of the big picture—our children need our love and attention more than anything. For example, stop trying to plan the perfect party games and actually play some games with your kids today. It's time.

JANUARY 13

"The LORD does not look
at the things man looks at.
Man looks at the outward appearance,
but the LORD looks at the heart."
1 Samuel 16:7

*C*omparing yourself with others is never a good thing, and it's not a God thing, either. God isn't concerned with whether or not your belly is as trim as it was before childbirth. He's concerned with the condition of your heart. Find your identity in Him. He loves you just the way you are.

JANUARY 14

You shall rejoice in all the good things
the LORD your God has given to you
and your household.
Deuteronomy 26:11

*D*aily aggravations will be a part of life until we get to heaven. We just have to learn how to deal with them. Here's the plan: Today if something goes wrong—stop, pause, and praise. Praise God in spite of the aggravation. Before long, the "stop, pause, and praise" practice will become a habit, the kind of habit worth forming!

JANUARY 15

As far as the east is from the west,
so far has he removed
our transgressions from us.
Psalm 103:12

*T*hank You, God, for wiping the slate clean. Help me to do better. Amen.

JANUARY 16

For as high as the heavens
are above the earth,
so great is his love
for those who fear him.
Psalm 103:11

*Y*ou've tried really hard to do everything right, but in the end, your best didn't feel good enough. Ever been there? On those days, I'm thankful that my heavenly Father is there to cheer me up. It's nice to know that He loves us no matter what—just like we love our kids.

JANUARY 17

Trust in the LORD with all your heart
and lean not on your own understanding;
in all your ways acknowledge him,
and he will make your paths straight.
Proverbs 3:5–6

*W*hen I was eight years old, I memorized the above scripture; it's still imprinted on my heart. Today, as the mother of two little girls, I encourage my children to memorize scripture, too. I know that those memory verses will pop into their minds whenever they need them most.

JANUARY 18

"Martha, Martha," the Lord answered,
"you are worried and upset about many things,
but only one thing is needed.
Mary has chosen what is better,
and it will not be taken away from her."
Luke 10:41–42

*W*hen I feel overwhelmed with the worries that accompany motherhood, I realize I've forgotten to figure God into the equation. God doesn't expect mothers to have all the answers, but He does expect us to go to Him for those answers.

JANUARY 19

Jesus answered,
"I am the way and the truth
and the life."
John 14:6

Getting lost used to really frustrate and frighten me. Now I consider it more of a fun adventure. I find that something good usually comes from it. You see, it's all in the perspective. Life is the same way. There's no sense worrying your way through each day. If we know Jesus as our Lord and Savior, we're on the right road because He is the Way!

JANUARY 20

Let us fix our eyes on Jesus,
the author and perfecter of our faith.
Hebrews 12:2

Lord, help me to keep my eyes fixed on You. Amen.

JANUARY 21

Dear children,
do not let anyone lead you astray.
1 John 3:7

I realize that I can't pick my children's friends, and I know that I can't protect them from the hurt that comes from broken friendships and disloyalty. But there are two things I can do—I can teach them about Jesus, and I can pray that the Lord sends them godly friends. You can do the same for your kids. You can start today.

JANUARY 22

"Love each other
as I have loved you."
John 15:12

*T*he Lord knew what He was doing when He put our families together. He knew that our kids would fight, and He knew they'd need each other. And here's another comforting thought—God desires for them to be buddies, too. So the next time your children are bickering, don't get discouraged. Just thank the Lord for His love in your home.

JANUARY 23

Many are the plans in a man's heart,
but it is the LORD's purpose that prevails.
Proverbs 19:21

The only way to control the stage mom in all of us is to realize that God is the best director. He doesn't need our input. He has a starring role for our children—if we'll only take our places backstage.

JANUARY 24

"Be careful, or your hearts
will be weighed down with dissipation,
drunkenness and the anxieties of life,
and that day will close on you
unexpectedly like a trap."
Luke 21:34

While there's no magic "worrywart potion" on the market, you have easy access to one that you might not have considered—God's Word! It will obliterate worry if you'll only believe it. God's got you covered. Worry never changed anything, but God's Word always does.

JANUARY 25

I know, O LORD,
that a man's life is not his own;
it is not for man to direct his steps.
Jeremiah 10:23

I often worry when we have to make big decisions concerning our children. I'm so afraid I'll stray from the path that God has for us, but you know what I've discovered? Even if we stray, God finds us.

JANUARY 26

"I, the LORD,
have called you in righteousness;
I will take hold of your hand."
Isaiah 42:6

*I'*m not sure why I neglect to reach for God's hand when I'm crossing the busy streets of life. I guess, like my daughters, I think I'm mature enough to handle it on my own. I'm so thankful that we have a loving heavenly Father who reaches down to take our hands when we need Him the most.

JANUARY 27

Look in the scroll
of the LORD and read.
Isaiah 34:16

*D*aily, I ask God to help me live out my faith. If my life is an open book before my girls, I want to make sure it's full of God's Word. How about you? Encourage your kids to read God's Word and then live your life according to His Word. That's a one-two punch against the devil!

JANUARY 28

Trust in the LORD forever,
for the LORD, the LORD,
is the Rock eternal.
Isaiah 26:4

*W*e want to make sure that our children don't think of God as a passing fad but as a steadfast part of their lives. To ensure that, we can feed them God's Word. We can also let our children see us loving God and His Word. Most importantly, we can pray that our kids will always love God—the real Rock.

JANUARY 29

"Therefore I tell you,
do not worry about your life."
Matthew 6:25

*F*ather, transform my thinking. Help me to quit worrying and simply trust You with every part of my life. Amen.

JANUARY 30

"Therefore do not worry about tomorrow,
for tomorrow will worry about itself."
Matthew 6:34

*A*s long as we're on this earth, there will be trouble. God tells us that in His Word, but He also tells us not to fret over it. That mean's it's actually possible to encounter stress and problems and still have no worries. The next time you encounter trouble, say "No worries!" and mean it!

JANUARY 31

Plans fail for lack of counsel,
but with many advisers they succeed.
Proverbs 15:22

We have a life expert always on the job—God. The next time you get overloaded with the cares of the world, call on Him. He will take care of everything, and He doesn't even charge a commission!

FEBRUARY 1

Satisfy us in the morning
with your unfailing love.
Psalm 90:14

Of course you always love your kids. But, if you're like me, there are days when you don't particularly love everything about them. At the end of those days I want to hit the rewind button and start the day over again, but it's impossible. God does have a rewind button, though! He lets us start over every time we fail.

FEBRUARY 2

"My grace is sufficient for you,
for my power
is made perfect in weakness."
2 Corinthians 12:9

Ask the Lord to help you see your children as God sees them. And ask Him to help you see yourself through His eyes, too. In other words, give your kids and yourself a break. Don't expect them to be perfect, and don't expect perfection from yourself, either. God loves you and your kids—flaws and all.

FEBRUARY 3

God is love. Whoever lives
in love lives in God,
and God in him.
In this way,
love is made complete
among us.
1 John 4:16–17

Life gets complicated, and families fall apart. It even happens to Christian families. But I'm here to tell you that love is the answer. Let God's love live big in you. Let God's love be the superglue in your family, binding you with one another for a lifetime. Live the love and reap the results.

FEBRUARY 4

*"Love each other
as I have loved you."
John 15:12*

*I*may not always get it right where my kids are concerned, but if my heart is right, God will cover me. He'll help me to show them just how much I love them. He'll do the same for you.

FEBRUARY 5

*Knowledge puffs up,
but love builds up.
1 Corinthians 8:1*

*F*ather, give me patience to love my children—even when they don't treat me nicely. Help me not to take it personally. Amen.

FEBRUARY 6

*"I have loved you
with an everlasting love."*
Jeremiah 31:3

We always tell our girls, "You are both our favorites!" Do you know that is exactly how God sees us! He doesn't love you or me more than anyone else—we're all His favorites! Meditate on that today and embrace the Father's love.

FEBRUARY 7

Love is patient.
1 Corinthians 13:4

Patience is one of those virtues that you admire in others but you're sure is not an option for you, right? Moms get a patience exam every day. I've often failed that test. That's why I'm so thankful that God offers "make-up exams." Through His Word and His unconditional love, we don't have to fail those patience tests anymore. The Lord can help us walk in love—even patience—if we'll only ask for His intervention.

FEBRUARY 8 ·

Do not let any unwholesome
talk come out of your mouths,
but only what is helpful
for building others up.
Ephesians 4:29

I've never owned an actual parrot, but I do have two little "parrots" running around my house. They repeat much of what I say, good and bad. Unwholesome talk and sarcasm really have no place in our conversations—not if we're living the God kind of love. So walk and talk love, and give your parrots something worth repeating.

FEBRUARY 9

[Love] always protects,
always trusts, always hopes,
always perseveres.
1 Corinthians 13:7

*O*ur children are faced with many challenges. Sometimes we're the only ones believing the best in them. We're the only ones on their side. Believing the best in our children doesn't mean turning our heads when they act inappropriately. Rather, it means giving them the benefit of the doubt. If we believe the best in our children, we'll get the best from our children.

FEBRUARY 10

Be imitators of God. . .
and live a life of love.
Ephesians 5:1–2

Valentine's Day is just around the corner. Love is in the air, so why not celebrate it? Steal some time away with your mate. . .let your children know how much they mean to you. Go ahead. You have an excuse to be mushy! Spread the love, share the love, and celebrate the love! And, by all means, eat a few pieces of chocolate, too!

FEBRUARY 11

Love is patient, love is kind.
1 Corinthians 13:4

Funny, I can practice patience and kindness all day long with friends, coworkers, and strangers, but some days I can't show my children the same love aspects. It's easy to act ugly, but it takes work to walk in love—especially with our children. Love is a choice. Choose to show your family love today.

FEBRUARY 12

I trust in God's unfailing love
for ever and ever.
Psalm 52:8

*B*ecause we use the word love so much, it has lost some of its luster and become clichéd in our culture. But real love—the God kind of love—is an everlasting love. It stretches as far as the east is from the west. It's deeper than the deepest ocean, higher than the highest mountain. It covers a multitude of sins. It is unconditional. God's love is truly awesome!

FEBRUARY 13

In the beginning
God created the heavens
and the earth.
Genesis 1:1

*T*he world's kind of love doesn't make the world go 'round. But the God kind of love not only makes the world go 'round, His love created the world. If your world is no longer spinning, run into the Father's arms right now. He longs for the opportunity to "love on you," in the same way that you adore loving on your children. Spend some time with the Father today.

FEBRUARY 14

"Love your neighbor
as yourself."
Leviticus 19:18

*L*ord, help me to love others the way that You love me. Amen.

FEBRUARY 15

Oh, how I love your law!
I meditate on it all day long.
Psalm 119:97

*A*s moms, we can't run on empty love tanks. We are expected to give love all day long. If your love tank is low today, pull up to the Word of God and spend some time with the Lord. His love is waiting for you, and it's premium stuff. Ready? Begin fueling.

FEBRUARY 16

A gentle answer
turns away wrath.
Proverbs 15:1

I recently saw a T-shirt with the words "Love is my final answer" printed on it. I thought that was pretty good. Think about it. When you answer with love, you give strife no place to go. Let love be your final answer today. It really works!

FEBRUARY 17

Show the wonder
of your great love.
Psalm 17:7

Do you have unstoppable love? Do you have the kind of love that overflows to everyone around you? I wish I could answer yes to those questions, but I'd have to say, "Not really." But we do have a secret weapon of love—Jesus Christ. Call on Him today. He can cause enough love to flow through you to totally soak your family.

FEBRUARY 18

[Love] bears all things.
1 Corinthians 13:7 NKJV

*E*xposing each other's shortcomings and failures is the exact opposite of love, because love bears all things. The word *bears* in that sentence means "covers." So the next time your little tattlers run up to you with some juicy information about another sibling, let them know that tattling and gossiping have no place in our homes. Let love root them out!

FEBRUARY 19

I trust in God's unfailing love
for ever and ever.
Psalm 52:8

*O*f all the people in my life, I want to make sure I show my kids unconditional, always-there-for-you love. When I fail to accomplish that goal, my heart hurts. But it's in those times that I sense the Father's presence in a big way. I can literally feel His love wrapping around me like a cozy sweater. No matter how many times I fail, God still loves me.

FEBRUARY 20

"I have loved you
with an everlasting love."
Jeremiah 31:3

"*I* love you more than a million red M&Ms." That's one of our favorite lines from the movie *What a Girl Wants*. My daughters and I have come up with a few of our own "Love you more thans. . ." Make today a day of love. Find new ways to say you love your children. Then have each child come up with a new way to express love to our heavenly Father.

FEBRUARY 21

[Love] is not self-seeking.
1 Corinthians 13:5

*G*od cares about your crazy, busy days. He knows that this "mom gig" isn't an easy job. He wants to give you rest and peace, and He is well pleased with your well doing. So the next time you hear "Mommy!" and you want to run the other direction—take heart! You are growing in love.

FEBRUARY 22

"Love your neighbor
as yourself."
Leviticus 19:18

*T*here are days I still have trouble with that love commandment. Sometimes I want to throttle my neighbor and repent later.
It's in those times that we find out how much love we have inside of us. When we are squeezed under pressure, if love is on
the inside, love comes out. But if we have other junk in there,
that comes out, too. So build yourself up in love. Trust me, you'll
need it!

FEBRUARY 23

"Man looks at the outward appearance,
but the LORD looks at the heart."
1 Samuel 16:7

*A*s our heavenly Father, God says no to some of our requests.
He sees hidden dangers that we don't. Occasionally I'll use that
old manipulation that never works—"You didn't answer my
prayer, so You must not love me." I'm thankful that God looks on
the heart, not the hurt. Show your kids that same mercy the next
time they say, "You just don't love me."

FEBRUARY 24

"Love your neighbor as yourself."
Leviticus 19:18

*I*t's hard to love ourselves. We tend to focus on all of our imperfections. If you are constantly belittling yourself, you need to get in the "self-love mode." Ask God to fill you up with His love and help you to see yourself through His eyes. When I look at myself through His eyes, it's like the best airbrush job ever! So love yourself today. It's not a biblical suggestion. It's a commandment!

FEBRUARY 25

But from everlasting
to everlasting the LORD's love
is with those who fear him.
Psalm 103:17

*T*his has now become one of my very favorite verses. To think that someone—especially the Creator of the universe—could love me for ever and ever is so great! What a wonderful promise!

FEBRUARY 26

"For I, the LORD your God,
am a jealous God."
Exodus 20:5

God wants us to love Him even more than we love our spouse and children. He wants us to remember those special times with Him—the moment you gave your heart to Him, the miracles He has performed in your life. Record what God does for you each day, a daily "love letter" to the Father. If you've grown cold to God, you're sure to fall in love with Him again.

FEBRUARY 27

"I tell you the truth, if you have faith
as small as a mustard seed,
you can say to this mountain,
'Move from here to there' and it will move."
Matthew 17:20

On days when I can't see even a shadow of love between my daughters, I continue to thank the Lord that it's there. Sometimes, I say it purely out of faith because there is no evidence of love. Put your faith to work, and watch the love grow in your home.

February 28

Love one another deeply,
from the heart.
1 Peter 1:22

*T*ake this opportunity to tell your children that you love them and that God loves them even more than you do—and that's a lot! Even if they wander from "the straight and narrow path," love will bring them back. God's love has a way of penetrating even the hardest of hearts.

February 29

"Look at the birds of the air;
they do not sow or reap
or store away in barns,
and yet your heavenly Father feeds them.
Are you not much more valuable than they?"
Matthew 6:26

*W*e would give our life for our kids, wouldn't we? Do you know that's how God feels about us? He adores us! He cares about each one of us. When we fall out of our respective nests, He is right there, hovering over us, protecting us, and loving us.

MARCH 1

You too, be patient
and stand firm.
James 5:8

*W*aiting is not easy, especially when you're waiting for something as monumental as the birth of a child. Even if you're waiting on God to perform a miracle in some other area of your life, it's tough. You wonder if God is still working on your behalf. But rest assured, He is! When you are able to finally embrace whatever it is you're believing God for, it will be more than worth the wait!

MARCH 2

"As long as the earth endures,
seedtime and harvest, cold and heat,
summer and winter,
day and night will never cease."
Genesis 8:22

*S*omehow that verse is comforting to me. Just knowing that God can keep all of the earth's functions in order, makes me feel good. I can rejoice in knowing that if God can keep the world spinning, He can certainly handle the tasks before me each day. The next time you're running in circles, call on Him.

MARCH 3

Jesus said, "Let the little children
come to me, and do not hinder them."
Matthew 19:14

I once read an article that said children spell love T-I-M-E. As I pondered that statement, I had to agree. Take advantage of each and every opportunity to do things together, going hiking, going fishing, doing crafts, reading stories, baking cookies, playing board games. . . . Don't just say you love your children—show them! Spend some time together.

MARCH 4

Be joyful always.
1 Thessalonians 5:16

*Y*ou may remember thinking, "I can't do this one more day! God must not have known what He was doing when He made me a mom." But, you know what? He did know. He has equipped you with everything you need to be a good mom. And He is more than happy to help you through when you feel your weakest. No matter what—God loves you and believes in you.

MARCH 5

"For I know the plans I have for you,"
declares the LORD, "plans to prosper you
and not to harm you,
plans to give you hope and a future."
Jeremiah 29:11

*F*ather, help me to fan the dreams You've placed within my children. Amen.

MARCH 6

He who heeds discipline
shows the way to life.
Proverbs 10:17

*G*od's time-out chair isn't a place where He puts you to punish you; rather, you put yourself there when you disobey Him. It's a place where the blessings of God no longer flow. But the best thing about God's time-out chair is that you can get up at any time. All you have to do is repent and move on.

MARCH 7

"Is not wisdom found among the aged?
Does not long life bring understanding?"
Job 12:12

*F*ather, as a sweet elderly man from our church once told me, these are the best years of my life. Help me to treasure each moment with my children. Amen.

MARCH 8

Let the wise listen
and add to their learning.
Proverbs 1:5

*A*re you a good listener? Do you really give your kids your full attention when they are talking to you? Do you nod your head and smile, letting them know that you're truly into what they are saying? If we fail to listen to them now, we'll be sorry later when they no longer choose to tell us things. Open up your ears and your heart and listen to your children!

MARCH 9

He gives strength to the weary
and increases the power of the weak.
Isaiah 40:29

Moms are busy people. That's just a fact of life. But if we allow ourselves to become too busy, we'll miss out on quality time with our families. We'll be running around so much that we won't know if we're coming or going. Even good things can be bad if they take us away from our families.

MARCH 10

Oh, how I love your law!
I meditate on it all day long.
Psalm 119:97

Soaking in bubbles totally de-stresses me and brings a quiet rest to my soul. Do you know what else brings peace and rest? Soaking in God's Word. When you spend time in the Word of God, it transforms you from the inside out. It replaces stress with peace; sickness with healing; anger with compassion; hate with love; worry with faith; and weariness with energy.

MARCH 11

*"But seek first his kingdom
and his righteousness."*
Matthew 6:33

One day it dawned on me—God is a great time-manager. I mean, hey, He made the entire world in a week! At that moment of revelation, I asked God to reveal the activities, volunteer positions, assignments, and friendships that needed to go. Then I asked Him to replace that "free time" with things He would have me to do. And you know what? He really knows what He's doing.

MARCH 12

*This is the day the LORD has made;
let us rejoice and be glad in it.*
Psalm 118:24

Life is difficult and traumatic events can uproot your entire life in an instant. So, we need to live each day mindful that these are precious times. Special moments with our loved ones are treasured times that are gone like the mist in the morning. Enjoy each moment with your children—even the not-so-pleasant ones—and thank God for the Kodak moments.

MARCH 13

*"By this all men will know
that you are my disciples,
if you love one another."*
John 13:35

*L*ord, help me to spend more quality time with my family.
Amen.

MARCH 14

*And pray in the Spirit
on all occasions with all kinds
of prayers and requests.*
Ephesians 6:18

*I*s your prayer life rushed and one-sided? If it is, don't despair.
Just begin spending quality prayer time with the Father today.
He's been waiting for you.

MARCH 15

The living, the living—
they praise you, as I am doing today;
fathers tell their children
about your faithfulness.
Isaiah 38:19

We're not promised tomorrow, which is why we need to live each day as if it were our last. Love a little more. Laugh a little more. Hug your kids more. Serve God with all of your heart. Make sure your kids know how much Jesus loves them. Think of today as a gift from God—because it is.

MARCH 16

Jesus said, "Let the little children
come to me, and do not hinder them."
Matthew 19:14

As moms, it seems our duty to say no. And sometimes, no is the correct response. But don't be so quick to always say no, or your children will quit asking you stuff. They'll go into their survival mode and put up their defenses. As moms, we should take time to really listen to our kids' requests before saying no.

MARCH 17

"Do not judge,
or you too will be judged."
Matthew 7:1

*T*aking time to know your kids and their likes and dislikes is very cool. It brings you closer to them. It puts you right in the middle of their world and helps you better understand their turf, their dreams, their struggles, and more. It's exciting and fun. And, you might just find out that you really like that Sponge Bob guy after all. (It's okay; I'll never tell.)

MARCH 18

"I have swept away your offenses
like a cloud, your sins like the morning mist."
Isaiah 44:22

I wouldn't change any of the big decisions I've made, but if I could turn back time, I would spend more time enjoying my children instead of just caring for them. We can't turn back time, and there's no sense living in regret. God doesn't want us to do that. But we can begin correcting those things today. The housework will wait—time won't.

MARCH 19

Don't let anyone look down
on you because you are young.
1 Timothy 4:12

You know, we're never too old to learn, and sometimes we neglect to recognize the teachers living in our own homes. Our kids may be younger, but in some ways they are much wiser. Why not let your kids teach you something today?

MARCH 20

. . .that is, that you and
I may be mutually encouraged
by each other's faith.
Romans 1:12

By encouraging our children, we can give them the confidence to move toward their dreams, to conquer their fears, and to fulfill the destiny that God has for each of them. Sometimes, all they need is a little nudge and a soft, encouraging word to move forward. Sure, offering encouragement takes time, but it'll be time well spent.

MARCH 21

Be very careful, then, how you live—
not as unwise but as wise,
making the most of every opportunity.
Ephesians 5:15–16

Our youth group at church changed its name to "14:40" to signify that our kids are learning to follow God every one of the 1,440 minutes in every day. There may be minutes in our day that we wish we could do over, but God knows that we are focused on making the most of the minutes for the Master.

MARCH 22

Make the most
of every opportunity.
Colossians 4:5

Lord, help me to make my children feel loved every day—especially on their birthdays. Amen.

MARCH 23

And my God will meet
all your needs according
to his glorious riches in Christ Jesus.
Philippians 4:19

Lord, please work a financial miracle in my life that would allow me to spend more time with my family. Amen.

MARCH 24

Jesus Christ is the same
yesterday and today and forever.
Hebrews 13:8

Isn't it good to know that no matter if you're sporting a mullet, "The Rachel," or a classic bob, Jesus loves you? His love never changes. His Word is as current and applicable today as it was a century ago. Even if our clothing, hairdos, and musical preferences are considered "totally uncool" by our offspring, we can offer them the One who will never go out of style—Jesus.

MARCH 25

Man is like a breath;
his days are like a fleeting shadow.
Psalm 144:4

It seems like only yesterday that we were celebrating birthdays at Chuck E. Cheese. Now we're having boy/girl skating parties. What happened to those years? They sneaked past me when I wasn't looking. Wouldn't it be great if we could keep our children little forever? But we can't, so don't miss one moment of their growing-up years.

MARCH 26

"To God belong wisdom and power;
counsel and understanding are his."
Job 12:13

Are you a member of the "You've ruined my life" club? Ask God to give you understanding so that you can see things through your kids' eyes. Once moms and kids see things through the other's eyes, understanding comes.

MARCH 27

"But my salvation will last forever,
my righteousness will never fail."
Isaiah 51:6

*W*e treasure those monumental moments, such as graduation day, our wedding day, and the birth of our children. But, do you know what the most special moment is? The day you made Jesus the Lord of your life. Make sure that you celebrate all of the special moments with your children. Most importantly, make sure that your children experience that most important moment so that they won't be searching forever.

MARCH 28

Finally, brothers, whatever is true,
whatever is noble, whatever is right,
whatever is pure, whatever is lovely,
whatever is admirable. . .
think about such things.
Philippians 4:8

*G*od, help me to help my children make good TV viewing choices. Amen.

MARCH 29

When you pray, go into your room,
close the door and pray to your Father,
who is unseen.
Matthew 6:6

Whatever your bedtime routine might be, I hope that prayer is part of it. Saying a bedtime prayer with your children is one of the most important things you can do for them. It teaches them to pray by hearing you pray aloud, gives prayer a place of importance in their lives, makes prayer a habit, and draws the family unit closer.

MARCH 30

Remember the days of old; consider
the generations long past.
Deuteronomy 32:7

Do you ever take a stroll down memory lane and take your kids with you? If not, you might want to put on your mental walking shoes and head down that path. More than anything else, it establishes a line of communication that wasn't there before. It gives you common ground. Go ahead. Share some funny stories from your youth. Your kids will love it.

MARCH 31

"If it is the Lord's will,
we will live and do this or that."
James 4:15

There are times when those to-do lists serve us well, and there are other times when we need to crumple them up and toss them into the trash. Don't be too busy with life to enjoy life. It's all about prioritizing, really.

APRIL 1

For where envy
and self-seeking exist,
confusion and every evil thing
are there.
James 3:16 NKJV

Lord, help me to keep my eyes on You and not on my short-comings. I repent for feeling jealous sometimes. Amen.

APRIL 2

"Come to me, all you who are weary
and burdened, and I will give you rest."
Matthew 11:28

We're moms. It's only natural that we desire to give our children the best. So it's no wonder we sign them up for all of these wonderful extracurricular opportunities. But be careful. They only get one childhood. Ask God to help you enhance their growing-up years without overwhelming them with "stuff." Even good stuff, if there's too much of it, can be bad.

APRIL 3

I can do everything through him
who gives me strength.
Philippians 4:13

Until we get to heaven, we're going to fail. We're going to have bad days. We're human! I think, as moms, we sometimes forget that fact. We set such high standards for ourselves—so high that they are unattainable by humans. If you've been feeling lower than a snake's belly lately, take heart! God loves you. Repent for your wrong-doings and ask Him to help you do better today.

APRIL 4

Aim for perfection, listen to my appeal,
be of one mind, live in peace.
And the God of love and peace will be with you.
2 Corinthians 13:11

One inspirational author defines "Christian perfection" like this: "loving God with all our heart, mind, soul, and strength." Now that seems doable to me. In other words, I don't always have to "get it right," but if my heart is right and if I'm truly seeking God, I can walk in Christian perfection.

APRIL 5

You need to persevere
so that when you have done the will of God,
you will receive what he has promised.
Hebrews 10:36

Striving for perfection is a painful process no matter if you're trying to achieve the perfect body or the perfect walk with God. Perfection is a myth, really. We are made perfect through Christ Jesus—not through working it as hard as we can. If we keep our eyes on Jesus, He will cause us to succeed.

APRIL 6

"I have loved you with an everlasting love."
Jeremiah 31:3

I absolutely love the quirky things about my kids. Do you know that God feels the same way about you and your little quirky habits? He loves you—everything about you—period! So many people feel they have to become perfect before God will ever accept them, but that's simply not true. When the Father looks down at us, all He sees is the Jesus inside of us, and Jesus is pure perfection.

APRIL 7

In the same way,
the Spirit helps us in our weakness.
Romans 8:26

W hen it came time to have my children, there was no mandatory parenting class. I felt pretty inadequate to fill the "mommy shoes." I discovered that I had to quit focusing on my inabilities as a mother and begin focusing on my abilities. God had chosen me to be a mom, and if He had chosen me, I knew that He had equipped me. He has equipped you, too!

APRIL 8

Each one should test his own actions.
Then he can take pride in himself,
without comparing himself to somebody else.
Galatians 6:4

One day while I was wishing I was more creative at baking birthday cakes, the Lord convicted me. God wanted me to know that He had given me special abilities that He hadn't given anyone else. Once I grasped that concept, I no longer felt incompetent. Now I can order Wal-Mart cakes for my children with great joy!

APRIL 9

For we are God's workmanship,
created in Christ Jesus to do good works,
which God prepared in advance for us to do.
Ephesians 2:10

I've always loved this scripture. Did you know that the word workmanship indicates an ongoing process? If we are God's workmanship, we are God's ongoing project. In other words, He isn't finished with us yet! Isn't that good news? I am so glad! I'd hate to think that I was as good as I was going to get.

APRIL 10

"Before I formed you in the womb I knew you,
before you were born I set you apart."
Jeremiah 1:5

Isn't it amazing how much you loved the baby you were carrying even though you'd never actually met that little person? To think that God knew me before I was ever born—wow! One translation says that God knew me and approved me. If you are struggling with a poor self-image today, snap out of it! You've been approved by Almighty God!

APRIL 11

So also the tongue is a small thing,
but what enormous damage it can do.
James 3:5 TLB

Thank You, God, for protecting my children from wrong thinking. Amen.

APRIL 12

*A heart at peace gives
life to the body.*
Proverbs 14:30

Are you at peace with the person God made you to be? You may not be happy with every aspect of yourself, but you need to be happy about the basic person that God created you to be. When you start practicing that mindset, your peace will return. And that's a great way to live!

APRIL 13

*Be strong and take heart,
all you who hope in the LORD.*
Psalm 31:24

Do you ever wake up and think, "Forget it! I'm not even going to try anymore!"? A better way to handle those days when stress and feelings of inadequacy try to overtake us is to run to Jesus. Some people forget that Jesus is Lord over every part of our lives—even the stressful parts. He has already gone before us, ensuring our victory. Rejoice! Be strong! Take heart!

APRIL 14

*Therefore, if anyone is in Christ,
he is a new creation; the old has gone,
the new has come!*
2 Corinthians 5:17

God is so masterful that He can take our old lives and transform us into beautiful creatures. Our once old and ugly hearts are revived, rejuvenated, and transformed by His touch. If you're in need of a heart transformation, go to the Master Designer. He's got a new look just waiting for you!

APRIL 15

*Whatever is true, whatever is noble,
whatever is right, whatever is pure,
whatever is lovely, whatever is admirable. . .
think about such things.*
Philippians 4:8

The Bible tells us to think on good and lovely things. God knew that if we thought on the other stuff for very long that we'd wind up in the self-pity pit. If you're in that pit today, reach up! God is reaching out to you, ready to help. Think on Him—not your past failures.

APRIL 16

I will praise you as long as I live.
Psalm 63:4

The devil knows what buttons to push in order to make you feel the very worst, but don't let him have access. When you start to compare yourself with another mother, stop yourself. Begin thanking God for giving you the wisdom and strength to be the best mom you can be When you respond to the devil's button-pushing with praise for the Father, you will send the devil packing.

APRIL 17

"God does not show favoritism."
Acts 10:34

I want my girls to know that God adores those things that make them unique and He thinks they are beautiful. I wish I'd learned that truth early on. As an adult, it's harder to accept God's unconditional love and approval. Yet, in my quiet time, I can hear God singing softly in my ear, "I love you just as you are. . ." Let God sing to you today.

APRIL 18

But the man who looks intently
into the perfect law that gives freedom. . .
he will be blessed in what he does.
James 1:25

Isn't it good to know that God doesn't expect us to be perfect? He understands that we are going to drop the ball once in awhile. We're human! He knows that because He created us. You're allowed to make mistakes. Whew! Good thing, eh? So relax. If you make a parenting mistake, God's got you covered.

APRIL 19

When they measure themselves by themselves
and compare themselves with themselves,
they are not wise.
2 Corinthians 10:12

Lord, help me to be satisfied with my best. Please give me a childlike perspective. Amen.

APRIL 20

Let us fix our eyes on Jesus,
the author and perfecter of our faith.
Hebrews 12:2

Many times, I've become so self-absorbed that I've lost sight of the real mission. Do you do that, too? The Word tells us to fix our eyes on Jesus. If you have your eyes on Him, you'll remain focused on the mission—not yourself. Where are your eyes today?

APRIL 21

I can do everything through
him who gives me strength.
Philippians 4:13

The God in me can accomplish things even bigger than I could ever dream. The God in you can do "big, huge" things, too. So get your big, huge faith on, and go after those dreams! Chances are, God placed those dreams in your heart, so He will help you accomplish them. You've got big dreams and a big God—that's a powerful combination!

APRIL 22

But thanks be to God!
He gives us the victory
through our Lord Jesus Christ.
1 Corinthians 15:57

There are days when my children come dragging in from school and I can tell that they've encountered some "yucky stuff" that day. That's when we as moms can speak life into them—just like our heavenly Father does for us. We can restore, revive, rev up, and send them back out ready to go.

APRIL 23

Do you not know that in a race
all the runners run, but only one gets the prize?
Run in such a way as to get the prize.
1 Corinthians 9:24

God doesn't expect you to be the best in every situation. He just expects you to do your best every time. Like the Bible says, press toward the mark. Then, even if you don't get the prize, you'll be able to hear God whisper, "Well done, my good and faithful servant."

APRIL 24

To all perfection I see a limit;
but your commands are boundless.
Psalm 119:96

You know the problem with trying to be perfect? You always end up disappointed in yourself and others. When I get in that perfectionist mode, I not only find fault with everything I do, but also with everything that others do. We need to give ourselves and others a break. Take your eyes off of your shortcomings, stop finding fault with others, and look to God.

APRIL 25

We all stumble in many ways.
If anyone is never at fault in what he says,
he is a perfect man.
James 3:2

I'm so thankful that God chooses to use imperfect people to accomplish His will on this earth. We are all a work in progress. Thank the Lord, He knows our limitations and He still loves us. No matter what kind of day we're having, God can still use us!

APRIL 26

But he said to me, "My grace is sufficient for you,
for my power is made perfect in weakness."
Therefore I will boast all the more gladly
about my weaknesses,
so that Christ's power may rest on me.
2 Corinthians 12:9

*I*f we let our children see our shortcomings, they'll feel better about their own weaknesses. Quit trying to disguise your weaknesses or make excuses for them. Just admit you've got them and let God's power be made perfect in them.

APRIL 27

Every good and perfect gift is from above,
coming down from the Father of the heavenly lights,
who does not change like shifting shadows.
James 1:17

*Y*ou are blessed. Send up praise to the Father for your children, your spouse, your home, your extended family, your friends. God loves sending blessings our way—especially when we appreciate the ones He's already sent.

APRIL 28

There is no fear in love.
But perfect love drives out fear.
1 John 4:18

God, our Father, wants us to run to Him when we're fearful. He wants to cast that fear right out of our hearts. If you're struggling with fears of inadequacy, if you're worried about your children to the point that your stomach is in knots—run to God! Let Him replace your fear with His perfect love. Now that's a deal you can't refuse!

APRIL 29

Clothe yourselves with. . .
patience.
Colossians 3:12

Have you noticed that everybody seems to have an opinion about how to raise children? Many times you'll receive parenting advice from your own mother—whether you ask for it or not. Before you verbally attack your mom the next time she offers a "helpful suggestion," pray. Ask God to help you receive everyone's input with graciousness and gratitude. Someday, you'll be the one dishing out advice. It's true, you know. We do become our mothers!

APRIL 30

"As for God, his way is perfect;
the word of the LORD is flawless.
He is a shield for all who take refuge in him."
2 Samuel 22:31

While it's a catchy phrase, "it's my way or the highway!" is not very correct in God's eyes. God's way is WAY more effective. If you're trying to handle everything on your own today—don't! Ask God for divine intervention. His way is best. After all, He is the Way!

MAY 1

You should praise the LORD for his love
and for the wonderful things
he does for all of us.
Psalm 107:21 CEV

I love to bless my children. You know, God is the same way. He loves to surprise us with the desires of our hearts. But He also expects us to acknowledge His blessings and have grateful hearts. Make sure the next time the Father sends down a blessing, you immediately stop and thank Him. He is worthy to be praised!

May 2

Give thanks to the LORD, for he is good;
his love endures forever.
Psalm 107:1

When something good happens to you, don't thank your lucky stars or thank goodness—they didn't have anything to do with it! Thank your loving heavenly Father who lavishly blesses us every day. Make thanking God a habit, and you'll find that you have many reasons to praise Him. It puts you in an attitude of gratitude, and that's a great place to be!

May 3

Great peace have they who love your law,
and nothing can make them stumble.
Psalm 119:165

Did you know that God's Word contains approximately seven thousand promises in its pages? It has promises to cover any circumstance or problem that you'll ever encounter. No matter what is going on in your life today, you can find a promise in His Word, something solid to stand on and build your faith upon. Praise God for His promises today.

MAY 4

And do not forget to do good
and to share with others,
for with such sacrifices God is pleased.
Hebrews 13:16

I sometimes act the same way with God that my daughters act with me. God will give me a huge blessing, and I'll rejoice for awhile, but two days later, I am whining around about how God has forgotten me simply because something didn't work out exactly as I'd desired.

Lord, help me to never forget Your goodness. Amen.

MAY 5

I urge, then, first of all, that requests, prayers,
intercession and thanksgiving be made for everyone—
for kings and all those in authority,
that we may live peaceful and
quiet lives in all godliness and holiness.
1 Timothy 2:1–2

T he tragedy of September 11, 2001 has given me greater appreciation for the blessings of freedom. Let's thank God for His covering over this nation and praise Him that we can worship Him without fear. And let's encourage our kids to do the same.

MAY 6

*"But seek first his kingdom and his righteousness,
and all these things will be given to you as well."*
Matthew 6:33

*I*f we seek God first, all of our wants will be fulfilled. But if we raise little "gimme" kids, they'll carry that mentality over into their relationship with God. Their prayers will be filled with, "Hi, God. Gimme this and gimme that. Amen." Ask God to get the "gimmes" out of your household today. That's one request He'll be happy to fulfill!

MAY 7

*A man of many companions
may come to ruin, but there is a friend
who sticks closer than a brother.*
Proverbs 18:24

*S*ometimes being a mom is a lonely gig. Toddlers don't leave much time for building close relationships. When I cried out to God for a friend, I heard that still, small voice say, "I'm your Friend." Wow. I'd totally forgotten that I had a friend in Jesus. If you're feeling isolated today—look up. You've got a friend in Him.

MAY 8

That my heart may sing to you
and not be silent. O LORD my God,
I will give you thanks forever.
Psalm 30:12

The best way to teach our kids to have thankful hearts toward our heavenly Father is by example. If they see us—their moms—praising God and acknowledging His goodness in everyday life, they'll follow our lead. Take time to not only teach the manner part of "thank you," but also teach the heart part of "thank you."

MAY 9

They were also to stand every morning
to thank and praise the LORD.
They were to do the same in the evening.
1 Chronicles 23:30

Lord, thank You for another day to praise You. Amen.

MAY 10

Give thanks to the LORD,
call on his name;
make known among the nations
what he has done.
1 Chronicles 16:8

*D*id you know there are several places in the Bible where we are instructed to tell what God has done for us? When God blesses us, we need to shout it from the rooftops. Encourage your children to share their praise. You might even schedule a time each week for "Family Praise Reports." It could be fun, and God will love it!

MAY 11

Praise the LORD.
Give thanks to the LORD, for he is good;
his love endures forever.
Psalm 106:1

*W*hen my girls were really little, I used to listen to them pray at night. They thanked God for everything under the sun. But, you know, besides being cute, our children's prayers should be a model for our grown-up prayers. When they count their blessings, they really count their blessings.

MAY 12

You are my God, and I will give you thanks;
you are my God, and I will exalt you.
Psalm 118:28

When I think about my earthly father, I always smile. My dad is the kind of dad who dotes on his children. But I don't love my dad because he is good to me. I love my dad simply because he is Dad. We should love our heavenly Father for that very same reason—just for being Him.

MAY 13

Let us come before him with thanksgiving
and extol him with music and song.
Psalm 95:2

Over and over in the Old Testament, God sent "the praise and worship team" ahead of the troops, singing and playing music unto the Lord. Obviously, God was trying to communicate that praise and worship are very important. When we praise Him—especially in the bad times—we ensure our victory. If you're in need of a victory today, praise the Lord!

MAY 14

Let the word of Christ dwell in you richly
as you teach and admonish one another
with all wisdom,
and as you sing psalms,
hymns and spiritual songs
with gratitude in your hearts to God.
Colossians 3:16

The phrase "with gratitude in your heart" appears many times in scripture. Just saying "thank you" to God isn't enough. Our hearts have to be filled with gratitude. We may fool our families and friends with false gratitude, but God looks on the heart.

MAY 15

Always [give] thanks
to God the Father for everything.
Ephesians 5:20

Father, help me to always have a grateful spirit. Help me to be an example for You. Amen.

MAY 16

"But be sure to fear the LORD
and serve him faithfully with all your heart;
consider what great things he has done for you."
1 Samuel 12:24

I encourage you to begin keeping a prayer and praise journal, maybe a family journal so the kids can participate, too. You'll be surprised how often God comes through in a big way. We just tend to forget unless we've recorded it somewhere. So celebrate God and look what He has done!

MAY 17

Why, you do not even know
what will happen tomorrow.
What is your life?
You are a mist that appears
for a little while and then vanishes.
James 4:14

*N*ot long ago, our pastor posed this question: "If you were told you only had a week left to live, what would you do?" As I was contemplating this, he continued, "So why wait? Go ahead and do those thing now." Go ahead. Live today like it's your last, because someday it will be.

MAY 18

Consider it pure joy, my brothers,
whenever you face trials of many kinds.
James 1:2

*W*e should be looking for reasons to be thankful—even in the stuff that would not ordinarily fill our hearts with gratitude. And, we should impart that same attitude into our kids. They'll be much happier children if they'll take that stance in life. It's really about looking for the silver lining in every gray cloud. Find that silver lining today.

MAY 19

We were not looking for praise from men,
not from you or anyone else.
1 Thessalonians 2:6

*B*eing a people pleaser is not only exhausting but also very pointless. First of all, you'll never be able to please everyone. And secondly, if you're doing things for people just to gain their adoration and approval, your motivation is wrong. Even if no one ever recognizes your good deeds, take heart—God knows. He's keeping track. And He thinks you're great!

MAY 20

*Be kind and compassionate
to one another.*
Ephesians 4:32

The grumpy shoe-store clerk was obviously having a hard day. And when she made a mistake in my transaction, she huffed and scowled when I pointed it out. So I made it my mission to encourage her. I thanked her for redoing my receipt. I praised her for her efficiency. We ended up having a nice conversation. She even smiled. Make it your mission to appreciate someone today. Start with your kids!

MAY 21

A friend loves at all times.
Proverbs 17:17

We busy moms rarely take time for our friends. But we need friends. If you haven't taken time lately to tell your friends how much you appreciate them, why not tell them today? While you're at it, tell your children how much you value their friendship, too. As my girls get older, I realize how blessed I am to have their friendship. Go ahead, reach out to a friend today.

MAY 22

I will proclaim the name of the LORD.
Oh, praise the greatness of our God!
Deuteronomy 32:3

"*P*raise and be raised, or complain and remain." When we praise God during the dark times, we're telling God that we trust Him—even though we can't see the daylight. And it's during those valley times that we truly feel God's tender mercy and experience extreme spiritual growth. So praise God today. Through your praise, you open the door for God to work in your life.

MAY 23

"How long will this wicked community
grumble against me? I have heard
the complaints of these grumbling Israelites."
Numbers 14:27

*H*ave you read about Israel's forty-year journey to the Promised Land? Actually, that journey should've only taken them about forty days. Their complaining made them their own worst enemy. Complaining is aggravating to God as well as to us. Let's keep teaching gratitude. Our kids will finally get it, or they'll have to stay in their room for forty years!

MAY 24

"Now, our God, we give you thanks,
and praise your glorious name."
1 Chronicles 29:13

*W*hy not take some time today to remember the times God has come through for you and thank Him for them? It's a trip down memory lane worth taking!

MAY 25

You should praise the LORD
for his love and for the wonderful things
he does for all of us.
Psalm 107:21 CEV

*I*t's good to be bold for Jesus, to communicate what we truly believe in and cherish. Make testifying a habit in your household. Lord, help me to be bold for You. I praise You. Amen.

MAY 26

Then Jesus looked up and said,
"Father, I thank you that
you have heard me."
John 11:41

*I*totally understand why Jesus wants us to come to Him like little children. When kids pray, they have no doubt that God hears their requests and will answer them. That's how we all ought to pray. Go ahead. . .talk to God. Tell Him your dreams, setbacks, and heartaches. Pray in faith, and thank Him for hearing you. It will make all the difference.

MAY 27

God has given you [surpassing grace].
Thanks be to God for his indescribable gift!
2 Corinthians 9:14–15

*I*wouldn't want to live one second without God's grace operating in my life. When I mess up, I can run to God. I don't have to hide. In the same manner, we should show our children grace. They are going to mess up. But, if we show them grace, they'll run to us, not hide from us, when they get into trouble.

MAY 28

May the God of hope fill you
with all joy and peace as you trust in him,
so that you may overflow with hope
by the power of the Holy Spirit.
Romans 15:13

The Bible calls the Holy Spirit our Comforter. As a mom, there are days when I need comfort. That's when I turn to the Holy Spirit. He helps me know what to pray and leads me to scriptures that pertain to my circumstances. The Holy Spirit truly is a gift.

MAY 29

"Now, our God, we give you thanks,
and praise your glorious name."
1 Chronicles 29:13

Praising God and having a thankful heart changes us on the inside. While a negative spirit puts up roadblocks on "the blessing highway," a thankful heart clears the road! He's worthy of our praise! Get your kids involved. Think of lots of reasons to give thanks. Make it fun, and make a joyful noise!

MAY 30

He blesses the home of the righteous.
Proverbs 3:33

As much as we love to give our kids the desires of their hearts, it pales in comparison to how much our heavenly Father enjoys blessing us. Where do you think that desire to give unto our children comes from? God is the best present-giver. He loves to see us enjoying the blessings He sends our way. So enjoy your blessings today. By doing that, you're blessing the Father.

MAY 31

He who is kind to the poor lends to the LORD,
and he will reward him for what he has done.
Proverbs 19:17

We support a little girl overseas named Carmen. While we're not allowed to ship anything bulky, we can send small tokens. We've sent paper dolls and have been told she loves them. I want to have "paper doll thankfulness." I want to be grateful for even the smallest gesture or gift. And I want the same grateful attitude for my children.

JUNE 1

Then the LORD answered me and said:
"Write the vision and make it plain on tablets,
that he may run who reads it."
Habakkuk 2:2 NKJV

While my dreams may be different from yours, in order to see our visions come full circle, we have to keep them before us! God has placed dreams and visions on the inside of everyone. If you've lost your dream, ask God to reawaken it today. Then "run with the vision."

JUNE 2

I can do everything through him
who gives me strength.
Philippians 4:13

For a long time, I didn't think it was okay to have other dreams besides being a mom. I though it was selfish to want more. But I discovered that God had placed those other dreams and desires inside of me. Being a mom is the greatest gig we'll ever have, but God doesn't want us to limit ourselves. He can use us—even in the midst of motherhood.

JUNE 3

"If you believe, you will receive
whatever you ask for in prayer."
Matthew 21:22

Our heavenly Father gives each of us unique dreams, and then He equips us to accomplish those dreams if we'll only believe. That's what I love about Him. There is no dream too silly, scary, adventurous, or extreme for our God. It gives Him great joy to see us pursuing the ambitions He has placed within us.

JUNE 4

Where there is no vision,
the people perish.
Proverbs 29:18 KJV

No matter where we are in life—a mother of a newborn or a mom whose last child just graduated high school—we need to have a goal, a dream, a vision. If we don't, the Word says we'll perish. I don't think it means we'll perish physically, but we'll die spiritually. That's why it's so important to find out God's plan and keep the vision close to your heart.

June 5

Teach me to do your will,
for you are my God.
Psalm 143:10

A vision is a dream your heart comes up with before it ever reaches your brain. You see, the real dreams in our lives are birthed in our spirit—deep down inside of us. They are much more than passing fancies—they are of God. If you haven't let your heart make any dreams lately, ask God to show you the dreams that He has for you.

June 6

A heart at peace gives life to the body,
but envy rots the bones.
Proverbs 14:30

Don't worry when you see others getting blessed. In the midst of seeing everybody else's dreams coming true, we have to keep our hearts right. If we don't we'll never get to walk in our dreams. Keep your eyes on the Master, and He will make your dreams come true, too. God has more than enough blessings to go around.

JUNE 7

But those who hope in the LORD
will renew their strength.
Isaiah 40:31

*W*aiting. That's one of the toughest things we have to do as our dreams percolate inside of us. Have you noticed that God's timing never seems to be our timing? It doesn't matter how much we cry out to Him, our dreams won't be birthed until God says it's time. So, if you're pregnant with a dream, and you're tired of waiting—hold on. Your promise is on its way!

JUNE 8

Now faith is being sure of what
we hope for and certain of what we do not see.
Hebrews 11:1

*B*ig dreams require big steps of faith. That's not always comfortable, but it's definitely exciting. Remember Peter? He was the only one who dared to dream and stepped out of the boat. When he started to sink, Jesus rescued him. He'll do the same for us. God loves it when we get out of the boat and dare to dream.

JUNE 9

"Do not give dogs what is sacred;
do not throw your pearls to pigs.
If you do, they may trample them under their feet,
and then turn and tear you to pieces."
Matthew 7:6

Not everyone is going to embrace our dreams and celebrate our victories with us. Be careful whom you choose to let in your inner circle. Only share your dreams with those who will be happy for you and celebrate with you. Remember, you can always share them with God.

JUNE 10

God gives a man wealth,
possessions and honor,
so that he lacks nothing his heart desires.
Ecclesiastes 6:2

The dreams that beat deep within our hearts come from God! We don't need any expert to interpret their meaning for us. God is the originator of those dreams, so just ask Him. He is willing to share His wisdom with you. God wouldn't have placed those dreams in your heart if He wasn't going to make sure they came true.

JUNE 11

I can do everything through him
who gives me strength.
Philippians 4:13

Jesus said we should have childlike faith. We should be able to believe BIG when it comes to the dreams and ambitions that God has placed within us. God wouldn't have placed them there if He wasn't going to help us achieve them. So learn from your kids. Get back that childlike faith, and start believing.

JUNE 12

"If you have a message
of encouragement for the people,
please speak."
Acts 13:15

People are hungry for encouragement. They are tired of dream squashers. If you are surrounded by dream squashers, let me encourage you today. God believes in you. Ignore the dream squashers. In truth, they are afraid to believe, and they resent you for stepping out in faith. Pray for them, but avoid them at all costs.

JUNE 13

My guilt has overwhelmed me
like a burden too heavy to bear.
Psalm 38:4

Sometimes living out our dreams comes with a price. As a writer, I occasionally have to travel to promote my books. When I miss something important at home, I feel guilty. Then God reminds me that He is in control of my life. If you've been on a guilt trip lately, unpack now! Guilt doesn't come from God! Instead, thank God for the good things in your life.

JUNE 14

"Again, I tell you that if two of you on earth
agree about anything you ask for,
it will be done for you
by my Father in heaven."
Matthew 18:19

Remind yourself to dream. Let your mind dwell on your dreams. Share them with your children and allow them to share their dreams with you. Then, as a family, you can pray over those dreams every night. Finally, when those dreams begin to manifest, you can celebrate together as a family.

JUNE 15

Now to Him who is able to do far more
abundantly beyond all that we ask or think,
according to the power that works within us.
Ephesians 3:20 NASB

I still believe that God is going to do big things in my life. He has proven Himself to me time and time again. If you've never seen the power of God in your life, ask Him to show Himself strong to you today. He's just been waiting for you to ask.

JUNE 16

"You may ask me for anything
in my name, and I will do it."
John 14:14

*W*e need to quit wishing on shooting stars and make our requests known unto God. Tell your dreams to the Father. Let Him know your innermost desires. Wishing never got anyone anywhere, but prayer changes things for the better. Faith-filled prayer will change your situation. So go ahead. Pray about your dreams today—you don't even have to wait on a shooting star.

JUNE 17

*This is the confidence
we have in approaching God:
that if we ask anything according to his will,
he hears us.*
1 John 5:14

Sometimes, when I think about the future and how I fit into God's plan for my life, I think, "I can't do that! I don't have what it takes." And I'm right—I don't, but He does. We just have to know Him. Do you know Him? The One who made the stars wants to live in your heart.

JUNE 18

*Joseph had a dream,
and when he told it to his brothers,
they hated him all the more.*
Genesis 37:5

Lord, thank You for the dreams You've given me. Help me to know when it's the right time to share and when it's not appropriate. I love You. Amen.

JUNE 19

"Have faith in God," Jesus answered.
Mark 11:22

*I*want to be so full of faith that I am running down my dreams—not just chasing after them. But that kind of faith only comes from the Lord. We have to meditate on God's Word and spend time in prayer before we'll have the kind of courage it takes to launch out in faith.

JUNE 20

Finally, brothers, whatever is true,
whatever is noble, whatever is right,
whatever is pure, whatever is lovely,
whatever is admirable—
if anything is excellent or praiseworthy—
think about such things.
Philippians 4:8

*H*ave you ever talked yourself out of a blessing? It's called thinking too much about the wrong things. What is God calling you to do today? Be obedient. He doesn't call us because we know a lot. He calls us because we know Him.

JUNE 21

*The tongue also is a fire, a world of evil among
the parts of the body. It corrupts the whole person,
sets the whole course of his life on fire,
and is itself set on fire by hell.*
James 3:6

*D*on't despise small lessons and small beginnings. Do whatever you're called to do now to the best of your ability. Just consider it preparation work for your dream—it'll be worth it!

JUNE 22

*"For I know the plans I have for you,"
declares the LORD,
"plans to prosper you and not to harm you,
plans to give you hope and a future."*
Jeremiah 29:11

*W*e need to know that God thinks we're special and that He has awesome plans for us. Even if your life has been difficult up to now, that doesn't change the fact—God has a special plan for you. Begin to thank God, and then watch as He unfolds His plan.

JUNE 23

I gave you milk, not solid food,
for you were not yet ready for it. Indeed,
you are still not ready.
1 Corinthians 3:2

Do you know that God doesn't dangle carrots just to tease us? He would be an unjust God if He placed a dream in our hearts with no intention of helping us achieve it. If you haven't yet realized your dream, it's not that God has forgotten you—you just may not be ready yet.

JUNE 24

Let us draw near to God
with a sincere heart
in full assurance of faith.
Hebrews 10:22

If we can train our minds and hearts to stay focused on God's plan for us, we'll finally become that plan. We'll enjoy the things that God has had planned for us since the beginning of time.

JUNE 25

*For you did not receive a spirit
that makes you a slave again to fear,
but you received the Spirit of sonship.*
Romans 8:15

*D*o you worry that you're not good enough or talented enough to do the things that God has placed in your heart? We can't allow fear to dwell in our lives. Fear is the opposite of faith, so you can't be in fear and in faith at the same time. You have to choose. So choose faith!

JUNE 26

*"If you believe, you will receive
whatever you ask for in prayer."*
Matthew 21:22

I love to read children's stories that end in "...and they all lived happily ever after." In reality, our homes aren't always so happy. A good marriage takes work. A happy home takes work. But both are possible. We must base our marriages and our families on the Word of God. That's the only way we'll ever experience the "happily ever after."

JUNE 27

And he said: "I tell you the truth,
unless you change and become like little children,
you will never enter the kingdom of heaven."
Matthew 18:3

Children have the best imaginations. It's nothing for them to dream big dreams. God doesn't have to work through doubt and unbelief like He does with us. If we will dream without limitations like our children, God will be able to do big things with us. Go ahead. Let your mind become like a child, and dream.

JUNE 28

Great is the LORD,
and most worthy of praise.
Psalm 48:1

Are you grateful when God opens the doors to your dreams? Do you immediately recognize that He is the door opener, or do you credit your success to your own skill? Sometimes when God answers our prayers and promotes us to the places we'd only dreamed about, we forget to thank Him. Thank the Lord. He is the opener of the doors to your dreams, and He deserves our praise.

June 29

The fear of the LORD leads to life:
Then one rests content,
untouched by trouble.
Proverbs 19:23

Have you ever heard the expression, "Be happy where you are on the way to where you're going"? If you're always looking to the future with longing, you'll miss the good stuff going on right now. There are gifts all around. Enjoy this wonderful motherhood journey. Every moment should be treasured. You have to enjoy today before you'll ever really appreciate tomorrow.

June 30

The Master said,
"Martha, dear Martha, you're. . .
getting yourself worked up over nothing.
One thing only is essential,
and Mary has chosen it."
Luke 10:41–42 MSG

Today's kids are too busy for their own good, but what about us? Who do you think they learned it from? There's not much time to dream or meditate on the things God has placed in our hearts or thank Him for His goodness. But we need to make time. It is vitally important to our spiritual health.

July 1

Trust in GOD.
Lean on your GOD!
Isaiah 50:10 MSG

I'm so thankful that we have God to lean on during difficult times. Even if our husbands or our children or our friends don't understand our feelings and even if there's no one else around to lean on, we've always got God. He promises in His Word to never leave us nor forsake us. Go ahead—lean on Him. He will be your Friend.

July 2

Cast all your anxiety
on him because he cares for you.
1 Peter 5:7

*W*hen my friend had a stillborn baby several years ago, we were all devastated. There were no words to comfort her. The only comfort for her pain came from God's Word. The Lord was there for my friend and her family during this time. While I'll never understand why my wonderful friend lost her baby, I've come to understand one essential—God is there for us when we're hurting.

JULY 3

O LORD, hear my prayer,
listen to my cry for mercy;
in your faithfulness and righteousness
come to my relief.
Psalm 143:1

*T*here are days when I wonder if I'm cut out for this motherhood role, especially the days when my children yell, "I hate you!"
That will bring on the self-doubt in a big way. But I've learned a
better route—give it to God. He has all the solutions. He cares
about you. He wants to comfort you.

JULY 4

"If my people, who are called by my name,
will humble themselves and pray
and seek my face and turn from their wicked ways,
then will I hear from heaven
and will forgive their sin
and will heal their land."
2 Chronicles 7:14

*L*et's take this moment to thank God for America. Let's pray
for our leaders and the men and women who defend this country.
Encourage your children to pray along with you. Make it a habit,
not just today, but every day.

JULY 5

"For your Maker is your husband—
the LORD Almighty is his name—
the Holy One of Israel is your Redeemer;
he is called the God of all the earth."
Isaiah 54:5

I have a friend who is an amazing single mother. There are days, though, when she doesn't know if she can do it all. But she knows that she can trust God for everything in her life. I'm thankful for all that she is teaching me about trusting the Lord.

JULY 6

"Man looks at the outward appearance,
but the LORD looks at the heart."
1 Samuel 16:7

*E*ven if we can't turn back the hands of time, even if our faces have a few more lines than they did ten years ago, even though we're growing older—God still adores us. Go ahead and slather on those beauty creams, but make sure you spend time basking in God's presence through His Word and through prayer. That's the only true and lasting beauty treatment!

JULY 7

"No weapon formed against
you shall prosper."
Isaiah 54:17 NKJV

Lord, I need Your help today. Thank You for being my biggest cheerleader—especially when I need an extra boost of encouragement. Amen.

JULY 8

And the people, that is, the men of Israel,
encouraged themselves.
Judges 20:22 NKJV

Do you ever encourage yourself in the Lord? As moms, we encourage everybody else. But we rarely take time to encourage ourselves. The Bible says that you are fully able to fulfill your destiny. It says that you can do everything through God's strength. Stop focusing on what you can't do and start focusing on what you can do.

JULY 9

"If all you do is love the lovable,
do you expect a bonus?
Anybody can do that."
Matthew 5:46 MSG

*D*o you realize that we have golden opportunities to show love to others every single day? If we'll discipline ourselves and show kindness when we want to react rudely, God will reward us. This is especially true when it comes to our children. Make kindness a habit. You'll find that if you sow seeds of kindness, you'll reap a mighty harvest of kindness.

JULY 10

Gideon said to him,
". . .Look at me. My clan's
the weakest in Manasseh
and I'm the runt of the litter."
Judges 6:15 MSG

*E*ven though Gideon thought of himself as "the runt of the litter," God addressed him as "You mighty man of valor." God didn't see Gideon as a weak worm of the dust. He saw Gideon as mighty. God sees you as mighty and strong and capable, too! Ask God to help you see yourself as He sees you.

JULY 11

"And I tell you that you are Peter,
and on this rock I will build my church."
Matthew 16:18

God loves to use ordinary people to do extraordinary things. Peter was just a fisherman, but God called him "the rock upon which I'll build my church." If you're feeling like you're not cut out for this motherhood job, cheer up! God is using you to do extraordinary things for the Kingdom of God. And He has more extraordinary things in store for you!

JULY 12

For great is the LORD
and most worthy of praise.
1 Chronicles 16:25

We all encounter difficult parenting moments—embarrassing public tantrums and fits—but if we can keep things in perspective, we'll lead much more joyful lives. Don't let Satan steal your joy, no matter how ugly it gets. Just smile and praise the Lord for every parenting moment—good and bad.

JULY 13

And let us not grow weary
while doing good, for in due season
we shall reap
if we do not lose heart.
Galatians 6:9 NKJV

*D*o you ever wonder if you're getting through to your children? Well, take heart! It turns out they actually do listen to us and internalize some of what we say. So don't grow weary in teaching your kids. Some of that wisdom is getting in there—I promise!

JULY 14

"Get wisdom! Get understanding!
Do not forget, nor turn away
from the words of my mouth."
Proverbs 4:5 NKJV

*A*s if this motherhood thing isn't hard enough, people from all walks of life feel the need to share their nuggets of wisdom with you. When everyone is trying to tell you what to do, smile sweetly and nod, but go to God for answers. Advice can be cheap, but wisdom from God is priceless!

JULY 15

*"Do not sorrow, for the joy
of the LORD is your strength."
Nehemiah 8:10 NKJV*

Determine to become positive—for your sake but also for the sake of your kids. They pick up on our defeatist attitudes. Get in the habit of saying these confessions every day: "God has made me an overcomer. No weapon formed against me will prosper. The joy of the Lord is my strength." Before long, that dark cloud that's been blocking the Son is sure to move out!

JULY 16

*Whatever I have, wherever I am,
I can make it through anything in
the One who makes me who I am.
Philippians 4:13 MSG*

Keeping all of the balls in the air is tough. In fact, some days it seems practically impossible. But on those days, I look to God. He says I can do all things through Him, so I'm holding Him to that. You should do the same!

JULY 17

"Ask and it will be given to you."
Matthew 7:7

After I had my oldest daughter, I went through a bit of post-partum depression. Maybe you experienced that terrible condition, too. I remember feeling helpless, hopeless, and clueless. If you're feeling down today, look up. God is there for you. He has all of the answers you need. And He is ready and willing to impart that wisdom to you. All you have to do is ask.

JULY 18

For God is working in you,
giving you the desire
and the power to do what pleases him.
Philippians 2:13 NLT

Do you ever feel rebellious? I sometimes have a hard time being obedient. Maybe you have that same challenge. But here's the good news: Whether or not you realize it, God is at work on the inside of you. He is constantly fixing you so that you'll want to obey Him. Here's more good news: God is doing that same work on the inside of our children.

JULY 19

Never forget your
promises to me your servant,
for they are my only hope.
Psalm 119:49 TLB

When something devastating happens to one of our children, it's hard to go on. We're mothers. We're programmed to hurt when they hurt. That's when it's time to run to the Word of God. When you need God the most, He is there for you. And you'll find Him in His Word.

JULY 20

When I pray, you answer me,
and encourage me by giving me
the strength I need.
Psalm 138:3 TLB

Moms are fixers. While that can-do attitude works in our favor much of the time, it can also work against us if we become too self-sufficient. When we rely on ourselves, we take God out of the equation. Of course, that leads to total chaos, confusion, and ultimate failure. So put God back into the equation. He's got the strength and answers you need.

JULY 21

"Oh, that we might know the LORD!
Let us press on to know him.
He will respond to us as surely
as the arrival of dawn."
Hosea 6:3 NLT

One thing you can depend on is that the sun always rises. That's why I like this verse so much. It says, "As long as the sun rises, the Lord is going to be there for you." No matter what you're going through, God is there for you, ready to respond to your needs.

JULY 22

"But as for me and my family,
we will serve the LORD."
Joshua 24:15 NLT

Are your children serving the Lord? Have they made Jesus the Lord of their lives? If you have a wayward child, I know the heartache you must be experiencing. It may look like your child is rebelling against you and God, but keep believing. Have faith that God is working behind the scenes to bring your child into the Kingdom. Stand your ground and wait for a miracle.

JULY 23

For I am the LORD, I change not.
Malachi 3:6 KJV

Styles come and go. Fashion and hairstyles change from season to season and year to year. In this ever-changing world, I'm so glad that Jesus never changes. The Word says He is the same yesterday, today, and forever. Hallelujah! A relationship with Jesus—that's the one thing we can give our kids that will never go out of style.

JULY 24

The disciples went and woke him up, shouting,
"Master, Master, we're going to drown!"
When Jesus woke up, he rebuked the wind
and the raging waves.
The storm stopped and all was calm!
Luke 8:24 NLT

God will quiet the storms in your life, too. He doesn't always calm the storms in the way that we want or anticipate, but He will do it. All we have to do is have faith. So call on the One who can calm the storms.

JULY 25

How can I know all the sins
lurking in my heart?
Cleanse me from these hidden faults.
Psalm 19:12 NLT

When Jesus comes into our lives, He totally cleans out our "life closets." He replaces hopelessness with hope. He replaces fear with love. We no longer have to be ashamed of skeletons in our closet because Jesus has taken care of those. We are new creatures in Christ. Don't worry about those skeletons. Jesus adores you, and He makes no bones about it!

JULY 26

So let us come boldly to the throne
of our gracious God. There we
will receive his mercy,
and we will find grace to help us
when we need it most.
Hebrews 4:16 NLT

As a child, I thought I had to be good all the time in order for God to love me. That's a warped perception, isn't it? Let's make sure that our kids know that God isn't out to get them—He's out to love them.

JULY 27

In a race everyone runs,
but only one person gets the prize. . . .
All athletes are disciplined in their training.
They do it to win a prize that will fade away,
but we do it for an eternal prize.
1 Corinthians 9:24–25 NLT

Moms are running the most important race—raising our children. Sure, there are days when you'd rather trade in your running shoes, but hang in there! Keep feeding on the Word of God—that's your training food. The finish line awaits!

JULY 28

"There is no other god
who can rescue like this!"
Daniel 3:29 NLT

We serve a very big God—a God who is able to handle any problem. I want to challenge you today to get a vision of the vastness of our God. If you keep a journal, write down all of the problems you're facing today. Now, write these words over the top of your problems: "My God is bigger than all of these things!" We serve a big God!

JULY 29

And I sought for a man among them,
that should make up the hedge,
and stand in the gap before me for the land,
that I should not destroy it: but I found none.
Ezekiel 22:30 KJV

We all know that we need God, but have you ever thought that God might need us, too? He is looking for willing hearts to take the message of His Son around the world. As moms, we can do that in our own neck of the woods.

JULY 30

Let them turn to the LORD
that he may have mercy on them.
Yes, turn to our God,
for he will forgive generously.
Isaiah 55:7 NLT

One thing about children, they are pretty quick to repent. We could all learn from our children when it comes to quick repentance. When we're disobedient to God, it's best to go right to Him and confess our sin and move on. He wants us to run to Him, not away from Him.

JULY 31

The LORD is the everlasting God. . . .
He never grows weak or weary. . . .
He gives power to the weak
and strength to the powerless.
Isaiah 40:28–29 NLT

*I*t's back-to-school time, and I'm exhausted. How about you?
Being a mom requires that we take on many tiring adventures,
but being worn out doesn't have to go with the job description.
If you feel overloaded and tired today, ask God to supercharge
your engine. He's even got enough strength to get us through this
back-to-school season.

AUGUST 1

But no man can tame the tongue.
It is a restless evil, full of deadly poison.
James 3:8

*W*e need to speak good things to our children! We should take
every opportunity to tell our kids, "You can do it! You are well
able to fulfill your destiny! You've got what it takes! No weapon
formed against you is going to prosper! I love you, and God loves
you!" Use your words wisely. They hold the power of life and
death.

AUGUST 2

The mouth of the righteous man utters wisdom,
and his tongue speaks what is just.
Psalm 37:30

It's perfectly okay to admit you don't know the answer to a question your kids come up with. Just tell them, "I don't know, but I'll find out. God has all the answers, and He is willing to share them with me." It's good for our children to see us vulnerable sometimes. It's especially good for them to see us seeking God for His wisdom.

AUGUST 3

[Love] doesn't fly off the handle.
1 Corinthians 13:5 MSG

No mom can be perfect all the time. We all lose our tempers. We all complain. We all get grouchy. But God knew that when He created us. He knew our flesh would win out once in awhile. That's why He sent Jesus to save us from our sins, so we can repent for our grouchy attitudes and move forward in love. So get those grouchies off and let love control you today.

AUGUST 4

Every word they speak
is a land mine.
Psalm 5:9 MSG

*H*ave you ever wanted to say something so badly that you practically had to bite through your tongue not to say it? When we spew hurtful words, we can't get them back. They do damage immediately. Even when you say you're sorry, their sting remains. So do whatever it takes to keep the cutting comments from escaping your mouth. You may have a sore tongue, but your heart will feel good.

AUGUST 5

He traveled through that area,
speaking many words of
encouragement to the people.
Acts 20:2

I think all moms were born to be cheerleaders. It's our job to encourage our little ones. We need to tell them that they can do it! We need to find creative ways to tell them they are special and encourage them. They need our approval and affirmation, so let's be quick to offer it. Get out those pom-poms and become a super encourager!

August 6

Love never fails.
1 Corinthians 13:8

*T*here are many ways we can say "I love you." We can sneak little love notes into our spouse's and our children's briefcases and backpacks. We can verbally express our love every morning and every night. We can bake a cookie cake and write "I Love You!" on it. Be as creative as you want, just make sure you take time to express your love every day. Be an ambassador of love in your home.

August 7

"Therefore my heart is glad
and my tongue rejoices."
Acts 2:26

*P*raising the Lord is one of the best things you can do to encourage yourself. Even if you're feeling down when you begin singing, before long, your heart will be glad. This scripture says our tongues should rejoice, so let your tongue rejoice today. Let your kids see you rejoicing in the Lord, and before long, they'll join in. It's contagious!

AUGUST 8

*For out of the overflow
of his heart his mouth speaks.
Luke 6:45*

Unfortunately, children (tween girls especially) can be cruel to one another. As parents, we want our children to understand the power of their words and to choose them wisely. We want them to grow up to be kind and respectful of others' feelings. And they will if we continually remind them that saying ugly things indicates the presence of an ugly heart.

AUGUST 9

*"My lips will not speak wickedness,
and my tongue will utter no deceit."
Job 27:4*

It's easy to see that it's wrong for our children to lie. But what about little white lies that we encourage? Like when we ask our kids to tell the telemarketer that Mommy isn't home now. A lie is a lie is a lie. We need to be conscious of our words because our kids are paying attention. Let's make sure we're good role models.

AUGUST 10

May the LORD cut off all flattering
lips and every boastful tongue.
Psalm 12:3

*H*ave you ever known anyone who always has to "one up" you? The next time, simply take a deep breath, smile sweetly, and move on. Give your irritation to God. He can help you see that person through His eyes of compassion, because someone who is always "one upping" everyone else is a person with self-esteem issues. So take the high road and walk in love.

AUGUST 11

Go near and listen to all
that the LORD our God says.
Deuteronomy 5:27

*W*hen you pray, do you do all of the talking? From the time we're little, we're taught to pray, but very few of us are taught to wait upon the Lord and listen for His voice. Waiting and listening requires time, patience, and practice. God speaks to us through that still, small voice—the Holy Spirit—and through His Word. If we'll only be quiet long enough to listen.

AUGUST 12

Your boasting is not good.
1 Corinthians 5:6

While exaggeration is kind of cute in our kids, it's not quite so cute and harmless when we do it. God isn't pleased when we stretch the truth—because "stretching the truth" simply means telling a lie. The Lord has helped me in this area. He reminded me that I don't have to prove myself to anyone. He is already pleased with me. He is pleased with you, too!

AUGUST 13

"If you have a message of
encouragement for the people,
please speak."
Acts 13:15

As moms, we are constantly speaking words of encouragement to our families. But we need a little cheering every so often, too. That's why it's so important to surround yourself with positive people. Find friends who are women of faith, and be there for one another. Pray for one another. Love one another. And encourage each other with a "You go, girl!" now and then.

August 14

His mouth is full of curses and lies and threats;
trouble and evil are under his tongue.
Psalm 10:7

Do you know the best course of action when a troublemaker is hurting your child? Prayer. Of course, that's the last thing you want to do. But it's the only thing that will produce positive results. Pray for wisdom. Pray that the troublemaker finds Jesus. And of course, pray for your child's protection. Use your tongue in the right way. Prayer changes things every time!

August 15

Beautiful words stir my heart.
I will recite a lovely poem about the king,
for my tongue is like the pen of a skillful poet.
Psalm 45:1 NLT

Those "little poets" who call us Mom listen very carefully to everything we say—good or bad. It should be our goal to be more like Jesus every day. If we become more Christlike, then our mouths will be like the pens of skillful poets, writing good things on the hearts of all we encounter.

AUGUST 16

Timely advice is as lovely as golden
apples in a silver basket.
Proverbs 25:11 TLB

We can learn much from the godly women in our lives. Cherish their words of wisdom. And some day your children will look to you for wisdom—it's true! So make sure you have some wisdom to share. Treasure the advice that's been given to you, and more importantly, meditate on the Word of God. There's much wisdom waiting for you!

AUGUST 17

"Take to heart all the words of warning
I have given you today.
Pass them on as a command to your children
so they will obey every word
of these instructions."
Deuteronomy 32:46 NLT

Have you every read a scripture that you're very familiar with, but all of a sudden, it teaches you something totally new? That's the Lord teaching you. His Word is alive! Fall in love with God's Word. Get wisdom so you'll have wisdom to pass on to your kids.

AUGUST 18

In the morning, O LORD, you hear my voice;
in the morning I lay my requests
before you and wait in expectation.
Psalm 5:3

*H*ow do you start your mornings? Do you spring out of bed, praising the Lord with great expectation? Begin each day thanking God. It will take practice, but you'll get the hang of it. Let your children see you praising Him, and encourage them to join in. If you do, mornings around your house will be a lot brighter.

AUGUST 19

My brothers, can a fig tree bear olives,
or a grapevine bear figs?
Neither can a salt spring produce fresh water.
James 3:12

*W*e need to continually ask the Lord to put a watch on our mouths. If our children see us praising God one minute and hollering at them the next, they will be confused and disillusioned with the things of God. And God is also listening. We'll be held accountable for our words—all of them!

AUGUST 20

"Whoever would love life and see good days
must keep his tongue from evil
and his lips from deceitful speech."
1 Peter 3:10

*O*nce when I caught the girls in a lie, I told them that lying always has consequences. And even if I had never found out, God would always know. That got their attention. You see, they love God, and they didn't want to disappoint Him. Strive for honesty in your house. God will be pleased, and that's no lie!

AUGUST 21

Dear children, let us not love
with words or tongue but
with actions and in truth.
1 John 3:18

*H*eavenly Father, help me to show Your love to my family on a daily basis. I love You. Amen.

AUGUST 22

Do not be anxious about anything,
but in everything, by prayer and petition,
with thanksgiving, present your requests to God.
Philippians 4:6

Moms are prayer warriors. It's part of our job description. But, are your prayers effective, or are you canceling them out? When you pray about something, don't talk against it with words of unbelief. Use your words to speak life to your children and praise to the Lord. Get in the habit of speaking good things, and watch your world change!

AUGUST 23

Nor should there be obscenity,
foolish talk or coarse joking,
which are out of place,
but rather thanksgiving.
Ephesians 5:4

Sometimes, we say things without thinking. We don't mean to say them; they just come out before we can retrieve them. Run it through your Holy Spirit filter before uttering a single syllable. Ask the Lord to help you say only uplifting, encouraging, and wise words. Make sure your filter is turned on all the time, and help your children develop their filters, too.

AUGUST 24

*"For out of the overflow of his heart
his mouth speaks."*
Luke 6:45

When we get angry, we often say things we don't mean. But according to this verse, we actually speak what is in our hearts. That's a scary thought, isn't it? So here's the key: We need to store up more of God in our hearts so that when the pressure is on, godly words will flow out of us.

AUGUST 25

*My people are ruined because
they don't know what's right or true.*
Hosea 4:6 MSG

Teaching our children God's Word and His ways are the two most important things we can give them, because if they have that knowledge, they have it all! As moms, we can't always be there for our children. But if we've equipped them with the Word of God, they will be all right without us.

AUGUST 26

"So shall My word be that goes forth from My mouth;
It shall not return to Me void,
But it shall accomplish what I please."
Isaiah 55:11 NKJV

*I*f one word from God can change our lives, then I should be speaking His words into my children at every opportunity. If your children are resistant to the Word, just let your life show His love, and eventually they'll listen. God's Word will finally take root in their hearts and produce some radical results.

AUGUST 27

"Do to others as you would
have them do to you."
Luke 6:31

*R*emember those telephone company TV commercials that featured the slogan, "Reach out and touch someone"? Maybe you've been feeling like you'd like to serve the Lord in some capacity but you didn't feel qualified in any area. Well, you can use the telephone to call someone with encouragement, right? Ask God if this might be a way that He can use you, and begin reaching out today!

AUGUST 28

*"I know, my God, that you test the heart
and are pleased with integrity."*
1 Chronicles 29:17

As Christians and mothers, we should walk in integrity. Of course, we know it's wrong to lie, but there are other ways that we compromise our integrity. For instance, if you tell friends that you'll meet them at 10:00 a.m. and you don't show up until 10:20, that's a lack of integrity. Let's determine today to be people of integrity in every area of our lives.

AUGUST 29

*He replied, ". . . If you have faith as small
as a mustard seed, you can say to this mountain,
'Move from here to there' and it will move.
Nothing will be impossible for you."*
Matthew 17:20

I want you to notice something about this verse. It says that we have to say to the mountain, "Move." Those little utterances that roll off our tongues make all the difference. Go ahead, fill the air with faith-filled words and watch God go to work.

AUGUST 30

"Now go; I will help you speak
and will teach you what to say."
Exodus 4:12

God made your mouth. God made your mind. God made you exactly the way you are. He knew you in your mother's womb. He knew that you'd someday be a mother. In fact, He knows the number of hairs on your head. He has ordered your steps. So don't dwell in doubt—walk in faith.

AUGUST 31

He is our father in the sight of God,
in whom he believed—
the God who gives life to the dead
and calls things that are not
as though they were.
Romans 4:17

This principle will work every time: Call things that are not as though they were. God even changed Abram's name to Abraham, because Abraham means "the father of many nations" (Genesis 17). Call your children good names. Fill your home with positive words. It will make a difference.

SEPTEMBER 1

The fear of the LORD is the beginning of knowledge,
but fools despise wisdom and discipline.
Proverbs 1:7

We have to think "future minded" for our kids because they live in "the now." Don't be afraid to stand your ground. Don't cave in to the whining and begging. Your rules are for your children's own good—even if they don't see it that way.

SEPTEMBER 2

Know then in your heart that
as a man disciplines his son,
so the LORD your God disciplines you.
Deuteronomy 8:5

I find that many times as I discipline my children, the Lord takes those opportunities to teach and discipline me, too. As it turns out, I struggle with many of the same challenges that my children do—imagine that? It pricks a bit when the Lord disciplines us, but we'll never mature if He doesn't correct. So embrace correction.

SEPTEMBER 3

My child, don't reject the LORD's discipline,
and don't be upset when he corrects you.
Proverbs 3:11 NLT

*T*he Lord doesn't want us to be discouraged by His correction. He corrects us because He loves us. He knows all of our faults, and He wants us to get past them and grow up in Him. Don't argue with God or talk back to Him when He gently corrects you. Just think, you're one step closer to being like Him!

SEPTEMBER 4

A refusal to correct is a refusal to love;
love your children by disciplining them.
Proverbs 13:24 MSG

*T*he only parenting book that's truly needed is God's Word. This verse clearly states that it is actually a refusal to love if we don't correct our children. So, while Junior may not feel loved at the exact moment he is being punished, he is experiencing love. Don't be fooled by the world's way of doing things. God's way is always the better choice.

SEPTEMBER 5

Get the truth and never sell it; also get wisdom,
discipline, and good judgment.
Proverbs 23:23 NLT

*H*ow often do you pray, "Lord, I am seeking your discipline to-day. Bring it on." I can honestly say that I've never prayed those words. However, it might be a good idea to pray that prayer once in awhile. If we'll be quick to repent and seek God's discipline, we can move on with Him. So go ahead—ask God to bring it on!

SEPTEMBER 6

For these commands are a lamp,
this teaching is a light,
and the corrections of discipline
are the way to life.
Proverbs 6:23

*T*he corrections of discipline should be a way of life for us—not just on the giving side, but also on the receiving end. Through God's disciplining, we can become the best version of ourselves.

September 7

The rod of correction imparts wisdom,
but a child left to himself
disgraces his mother.
Proverbs 29:15

*T*here are lots of differing opinions about how to discipline our children. So what is the answer? God is the only true answer. You must seek His face and ask His direction. He will teach you how to discipline your kids. He loves them even more than you do. He will impart wisdom to you so that you can impart wisdom to your children.

September 8

A fool spurns his father's discipline,
but whoever heeds correction
shows prudence.
Proverbs 15:5

*D*id you know that parenting isn't a popularity contest? Yes, I want my kids to think I'm cool. Yes, I want them to think of me as a friend. But more than anything else, I want to raise my girls to love God and walk in His ways. If that means making some unpopular decisions, then that's okay by me. We'll always be popular to God.

SEPTEMBER 9

But the lovingkindness of the Lord
is from everlasting to everlasting.
Psalm 103:17 TLB

I'm so thankful that God is gentle, and merciful when He disciplines. He makes His children want to run to Him, not away from Him. No matter how badly we mess up, He forgives and forgets. If you are struggling with being too harsh with your children, ask God to help you. He will pour His unconditional love into you so you can pour that love on your children.

SEPTEMBER 10

For the LORD is good and his love endures forever;
his faithfulness continues
through all generations.
Psalm 100:5

*H*as God been there for you when no one else was around? Has He helped you make it through a difficult situation? Maybe you're in a tough place now and need His touch. Just reach out—He's right there. No matter what your situation—He has the way out. He is able. He is willing. And He is faithful.

SEPTEMBER 11

Do not boast about tomorrow,
for you do not know
what a day may bring forth.
Proverbs 27:1

September 11 will forever mean something different since the tragedy that struck America in 2001. If 9/11 taught us anything as a country, it taught us to cherish our loved ones. Take time today to pray for the families who lost loved ones on that tragic day. Pray for our nation and its leaders. And tell your family just how much you love them.

SEPTEMBER 12

If you are guided by the Spirit,
you won't obey your selfish desires.
Galatians 5:16 CEV

Did you know that we make approximately twenty-five hundred choices every single day? I don't trust my mind. I'd much rather rely on the leading of the Holy Spirit to make decisions—especially when it comes to disciplining my children. Don't reason and worry your life away. Instead, ask for God's leading to help you make the best possible decisions.

SEPTEMBER 13

Before I formed you in the womb I knew [and]
approved of you [as My chosen instrument].
Jeremiah 1:5 AMP

On those days when I feel like I'm losing this parental battle, it's nice to know that God has already approved me. No matter what, God loves me and sees me as a great mom. He always has His faith eyes in focus. Ask Him to help you get your faith eyes in focus, too. See yourself as God sees you—approved!

SEPTEMBER 14

Because the LORD disciplines those he loves,
as a father the son he delights in.
Proverbs 3:12

We discipline our kids because we want them to learn respect and obedience—because we love them. We know that if we don't discipline them, it will be detrimental to them in the long run. God does the same thing for us. He knows our potential, and if we'll let Him, He will mold us and make us into the moms He created us to be.

SEPTEMBER 15

Come, children, listen closely;
I'll give you a lesson in GOD worship.
Psalm 34:11 MSG

Make the most of every opportunity to teach your children about the nature of God—God the Healer, God the Provider, God the Savior, God the Deliverer, God the Great I Am! There are chances every day to share little lessons with our children. Ask the Lord to help you identify those opportunities so that you can take advantage of each one.

SEPTEMBER 16

Teach them to your children.
Talk about them wherever you are,
sitting at home or walking in the street;
talk about them from the time you get up
in the morning until you fall into bed at night.
Deuteronomy 11:19 MSG

As moms, we need to seize and embrace the opportunities to teach lessons. God will provide the perfect situations, but we have to be "tuned in" to Him in order to take advantage of these precious opportunities. Tune in today!

SEPTEMBER 17

He will die for lack of discipline,
led astray by his own great folly.
Proverbs 5:23

*N*one of us would intentionally hurt our kids. We love them. But sometimes we love them too much, meaning we don't discipline them for their wrong behavior. If we don't teach them right from wrong, they'll make wrong choices, which will lead to heartache, ruin, and ultimately, destruction. Our role is crucial. Ask the Lord to help you be firm yet loving as you discipline your kids.

SEPTEMBER 18

"Declare what is to be."
Isaiah 45:21

*I*f you are going to live a victorious life, you must speak positive words of faith and say what God says about your situation. Find scriptures to stand on—scriptures that fit your situation. Don't talk the problem—talk the solution. Trust the Lord to do what He says in His Word. His Word never returns void. It will accomplish its purpose. Get ready for victory—it's on its way!

SEPTEMBER 19

So do not throw away your confidence;
it will be richly rewarded.
Hebrews 10:35

When today has so many worries, responsibilities, and obligations, it's difficult to be future minded. But we need to make a conscious effort. We need to let God stir up our faith. We need to start believing God for big things. Focus on the future. See your children well and serving God. See your family happy and whole. Get a vision of victory today!

SEPTEMBER 20

"This vision is for a future time. . ..
If it seems slow in coming, wait patiently,
for it will surely take place.
It will not be delayed."
Habakkuk 2:3 NLT

Resting in God means trusting and not worrying. As moms, we need to rest and wait more than anyone else. If we're frazzled, we'll raise frazzled children. If we're impatient and worried, we'll raise impatient, worried children. So here's your assignment—rest and wait!

SEPTEMBER 21

Therefore put on the full armor of God, so that. . .
you may be able to stand your ground.
Ephesians 6:13

There are lots of parenting books and magazines with conflicting advice. But there's only one manual that covers it all. From disciplining your children to showing them unconditional love, the Word of God has got you covered. Need an answer for a specific situation? Don't rely on secondhand information. Go to the Manual. Read the Word and let it come alive to you.

SEPTEMBER 22

For these commands are a lamp,
this teaching is a light,
and the corrections of discipline
are the way to life,
Proverbs 6:23

Just think if we had an infomercial for the Word of God. We could make claims like, "Guaranteed to produce results! Never gets old! Full of the wisdom of the ages! Works every time!" and they'd be true! God's Word provides correction, healing, prosperity, joy, and wisdom through its many promises. No matter what you need, go to the Word.

SEPTEMBER 23

Have mercy on me, O God,
according to your unfailing love;
according to your great compassion
blot out my transgressions.
Psalm 51:1

Showing mercy to our children is a good thing. We shouldn't let them get away with horrible behavior, but we need to discipline in love and emulate our heavenly Father. Aren't you glad we serve a merciful God? We need to discipline our kids and teach them the ways of God, but we need to do so with love and mercy.

SEPTEMBER 24

It's the child he loves that he disciplines.
Hebrews 12:6 MSG

Before you discipline your child, find a scripture that pertains to the situation at hand. Then you will have all the ammunition you need to lovingly enforce discipline. It takes the pressure off of you and puts it on the Word, and God's Word can handle the pressure.

SEPTEMBER 25

Your obedience will give you a long life
on the soil that GOD promised to give
your ancestors and their children,
a land flowing with milk and honey.
Deuteronomy 11:9 MSG

*O*bedience is doing what you're supposed to do the first time you're asked. We shouldn't have to ask our children numerous times in order to get their attention. Let's ask God to help us teach our children the true meaning of obedience today.

SEPTEMBER 26

GOD is fair and just; He corrects the misdirected,
Sends them in the right direction.
Psalm 25:8 MSG

*I*n the spiritual realm, God corrects our course, puts us back on the right road, and points us toward our heavenly home. Without His gentle correction, we might head in the wrong direction our entire lives. If God didn't love us, He'd just let us wander around aimlessly. So thank the Lord today for His divine correction and direction.

SEPTEMBER 27

Don't be afraid to correct your young ones;
a spanking won't kill them.
Proverbs 23:13 MSG

I wish I never had to discipline my children. I wish they were perfect all the time. But since that's not the case, I have to take a disciplinarian stance from time to time. It's part of our job as mothers. We should never be afraid to discipline our children. We should be fearful if we don't.

SEPTEMBER 28

"Not all who sound religious are really godly people.
They may refer to me as 'Lord,'
but still won't get to heaven.
For the decisive question is whether
they obey my Father in heaven."
Matthew 7:21 TLB

O beying the Father should be high on our priority list and on our children's list, too. Obeying our God shouldn't be a difficult thing. If you're having trouble obeying Him, spend some quality time with Him. Make Him your first love, and obedience will soon follow.

SEPTEMBER 29

*"What stories you can tell your children
and grandchildren about the incredible things I am doing...
and how I proved to you that I am Jehovah."*
Exodus 10:2 TLB

*P*art of training up our children is sharing the miracles of God with them—the mighty works that God performed in the Bible, and also the mighty works He has done personally in our families. Hearing those stories builds our children's faith, and it builds ours, too.

SEPTEMBER 30

*These older women must train
the younger women to love their husbands
and their children.*
Titus 2:4 NLT

I've learned so much from my mother. Not only has she taught me about being a mom, but she's taught me how to be a better wife. There is much to be learned from our elders, isn't there? God will send wise women to be part of your life. Ask Him to do that for you today.

OCTOBER 1

"Give, and it will be given to you:
good measure, pressed down,
shaken together, and running over."
Luke 6:38 NKJV

One of the main ways you can guarantee joy in your life is by living to give. God promises to multiply back to you everything that you give. When you step out in faith, you open a door for God to move on your behalf. It's the simple principle of sowing and reaping. As mothers, we are super sowers. Get ready for a super huge harvest!

OCTOBER 2

"By this kind of hard work we must help the weak,
remembering the words the Lord Jesus himself said:
'It is more blessed to give than to receive.'"
Acts 20:35

As we approach the holidays, I worry about spoiling my girls. That's why I was so blessed to see that their hearts are as big as their wish lists. Not long ago, they heard of a local ministry's needs and they sprang into action. While my daughters love receiving, they also love giving.

OCTOBER 3

"So when you give to the needy,
do not announce it with trumpets."
Matthew 6:2

We were on a stakeout. Our mission? To deliver several Christmas presents without our single-mom friend ever finding out who delivered them. We had the best time choosing each gift, and sneaking inside her office to deliver them. That Christmas, the girls and I learned that it truly is better to give than to receive. We should look for opportunities to give unto others.

OCTOBER 4

Concentrate on doing your best for God,
work you won't be ashamed of.
2 Timothy 2:15 MSG

When it comes to being a mom, do you look for the easy way out, or do you go the extra mile? If you're like me, it just depends on the day. But God expects our best because, after all, He gave His best for us. He gave His only Son to die on the cross for our sins. Give God your best today!

OCTOBER 5

"You shall not give false testimony
against your neighbor."
Exodus 20:16

*A*s moms, it's tough to stand by and let someone say hurtful untruths about our kids. In one situation, I wanted to call the mother and give her a piece of my mind. But the Holy Spirit instructed me to give something else—love. Then the Lord gave me peace and the ability to comfort my girls. Let's make a decision to give only good things today.

OCTOBER 6

"I'll give him and his descendants
the land he walked on because he
was all for following GOD,
heart and soul."
Deuteronomy 1:36 MSG

I don't know why we'd ever want to hold out on God. He simply wants us to give our all so that we can walk in His plan. If you're struggling with giving God your all today, ask Him to help you. Let go and let God. He will give you much more in return.

OCTOBER 7

"Now I am giving him to the LORD,
and he will belong
to the LORD his whole life."
1 Samuel 1:28 NLT

*H*ave you truly given your children to God? We trust God with everything in our lives, but when it comes to our children, we want to take care of them. But being in the center of God's will is the safest place a person can be. Giving your kids to God is the best thing you can do for them.

OCTOBER 8

"Whoever wants to be first among
you must be your slave."
Matthew 20:27 MSG

*I*t's fun to hear the girls warm up for Honor Choir. They go through this whole "Mi. Mi. Mi. Mi. Mi." routine. But if you're living with the "Me. Me. Me. Me. Me." mentality, that's no good. If it's all about you, then it can't be all about Him. God has a good plan for you life—don't mess it up singing the wrong song.

OCTOBER 9

"'These people honor me with their lips,
but their hearts are far from me.'"
Matthew 15:8 NLT

Whether you are aware of it or not, you are constantly witnessing to those around you—especially your children. So do and say things in accordance with the Bible. Let God's light shine big in you. Let your mouth speak good things. Let your actions mirror the Father's actions. Walk the talk—no matter what. Ask God to help you.

OCTOBER 10

This is what the LORD says:
"Stop at the crossroads and look around.
Ask for the old, godly way, and walk in it.
Travel its path, and
you will find rest for your souls."
Jeremiah 6:16 NLT

Steal a few minutes today and retreat to the Word of God. The Bible isn't just some ancient history book. It's alive! Just by reading it, you'll feel more energized and hopeful. God will restore you. Spend time in His Word and find rest!

OCTOBER 11

"Give praise to the LORD your God!"
1 Chronicles 29:20 NLT

*P*reschool children have no baggage or inhibitions. They are full of life and love and laughter. And they absolutely love to praise the Lord! When it comes to making a joyful noise before the Lord, these kids have got it going on! Make praising the Lord a part of your daily life. Make it a family affair! Pretty soon, you'll be as proficient at giving God praise as the little ones.

OCTOBER 12

"Bring the whole tithe into the storehouse,
that there may be food in my house. Test me in this,"
says the LORD Almighty,
"and see if I will not throw open the floodgates
of heaven and pour out so much blessing
that you will not have room enough for it."
Malachi 3:10

*L*ord, help me to be a cheerful giver. Amen.

OCTOBER 13

"'The LORD turn his face toward
you and give you peace.'"
Numbers 6:26

*H*ave you ever asked the Lord to give you peace? I'm talking about the kind of peace that only the Father can give—even in the midst of chaos. The Bible says it's a peace that surpasses all understanding. In other words, it's a kind of peace that people don't understand. It's hard to put into words. That's the kind of peace that I want to walk in every day.

OCTOBER 14

He gives strength to the weary
and increases the power of the weak.
Isaiah 40:29

*E*ven if you can't say no, like me, you don't have to feel weary anymore. This verse says God gives strength to the weary and weak. I don't know about you, but I qualify! The next time you're feeling overworked and overwhelmed, just call on the name of the Lord. Ask Him to give you strength. He will do it every time!

OCTOBER 15

*"A new command I give you:
Love one another. As I have loved you,
so you must love one another."*
John 13:34

When we had kids, God literally increased our ability and capacity to love. Love is much more than an emotion—it's a state of being. And we should always be in love with the Father so that we can show His kind of love to our kids. Love your kids big today!

OCTOBER 16

*"For I know the plans I have for you,"
declares the LORD, "plans to prosper you
and not to harm you,
plans to give you hope and a future."*
Jeremiah 29:11

In life, you just can't plan for everything. But remember—while you can't plan for everything, God can. He has a plan for your life, so don't sweat the small stuff.

OCTOBER 17

For everyone born of God overcomes the world.
This is the victory that has overcome the world,
even our faith.
1 John 5:4

*T*he Bible says that faith comes by hearing the Word of God. As you hear the Word and store it in your heart, your faith grows stronger. Then, the next time the enemy tries to make you feel worthless, discouraged, depressed, worried, or overwhelmed, you can put your faith to work by declaring the Word of God.

OCTOBER 18

I will refuse to look at anything
vile and vulgar.
Psalm 101:3 NLT

*W*hile spending the night at a friend's house, my daughter recently saw a movie that she shouldn't have seen. Then she suffered with nightmares for weeks! Don't let fear and other negative material get into your children's hearts and minds. Be that filter for them. As a family, think on lovely things and give the devil no place in your home.

OCTOBER 19

For wherever there is jealousy or selfish ambition,
there will be disorder
and every other kind of evil.
James 3:16 TLB

*D*on't let strife take root in your home because you don't want to open up your household to every kind of evil. Instead, build your house on love. When your kids fight, nip it in the bud. Pray for peace, and watch your family transform. You can have heaven on earth in your home. Start today!

OCTOBER 20

"See, I am doing a new thing!
Now it springs up;
do you not perceive it?"
Isaiah 43:19

*T*his verse doesn't say that God is going to do a new thing in a year or two. It says He is doing a new thing now! So if you're in a faith rut, or if your kids are driving you crazy, or if you're fighting a weight problem, or if you're depressed—cheer up! God is doing a new thing for you.

OCTOBER 21

"There's hope for your children."
GOD's Decree.
Jeremiah 31:17 MSG

Are your children away from God right now? If they are, I know that you're heartbroken. But you must praise God for the victory even before it takes place. He has commanded that we live in victory, so that means no matter how bad it looks right now, you can be encouraged. We already know how it ends—we win! Praise the Lord today! Your victory is on its way!

OCTOBER 22

Gently encourage the stragglers,
and reach out for the exhausted,
pulling them to their feet.
Be patient with each person,
attentive to individual needs.
1 Thessalonians 5:14 MSG

Our children (and our spouses, too!) need our encouragement. They need our support and unconditional love on a daily basis. Of course, in order to have encouragement to dish out, we have to fill ourselves up again. We do that by praying, reading God's Word, praising the Lord—and by getting enough rest.

OCTOBER 23

*Let the Word of Christ—the Message—
have the run of the house.
Give it plenty of room in your lives.*
Colossians 3:16 MSG

*H*ave you given the Word a prominent place in your life? I used to think, "How can God expect me to spend time in the Word and get all of this stuff done, too?" But you know what I discovered? If I make time for God, He makes sure I accomplish all that is on my plate.

OCTOBER 24

*But those who wait for the Lord
[who expect, look for, and hope in Him]
shall change and renew their strength.*
Isaiah 40:31 AMP

*D*o you expect God's best for your life and your children's lives? Don't let your lack of expectations set limits for your life. If you never expect anything good, you're never going to receive anything good. Live every day filled with anticipation of what God is going to do in your life and your children's lives.

OCTOBER 25

Don't use foul or abusive language.
Ephesians 4:29 NLT

Do your children look for the best in people? Kids are brutally honest. Sometimes they are critical without even meaning to be.

Lord, help me to raise positive children—kids who look for the best in everyone. Amen.

OCTOBER 26

"Get wisdom, get understanding;
do not forget my words
or swerve from them."
Proverbs 4:5

No matter what you need today, you can go to God and seek His counsel. He wants you to! He wants us to hunger and thirst after Him. He wants us to seek Him. He wants to share His wisdom with us. Take your questions and concerns to the Father. He's ready, willing, and able to answer.

OCTOBER 27

He will not allow your foot to be moved;
He who keeps you will not slumber.
Psalm 121:3 NKJV

When I pray to the Father, I always picture Him sitting in a big, wooden rocking chair and beckoning me to sit on His lap. If you need to de-stress today, crawl into your heavenly Father's lap and rock awhile.

OCTOBER 28

"I will dwell in them
And walk among them.
I will be their God,
And they shall be My people."
2 Corinthians 6:16 NKJV

Are your kids independent? I sometimes feel as if my girls no longer need me and I'm not too happy about it. I bet that's how God feels when we try to do everything on our own without asking for His help or intervention. We should rely on God all the time. We can't make it even one step without Him.

OCTOBER 29

But the fruit of the Spirit is love, joy, peace,
patience, kindness, goodness, faithfulness,
gentleness and self-control.
Galatians 5:22–23

As Christians, we can have all of the fruit of the Spirit operating in our lives. We can claim that promise for ourselves and our children. Put Galatians 5:22–23 in action today. Why not offer to help someone or send a card of appreciation. Ask your kids to help you, and you can work on growing more fruit of the Spirit together.

OCTOBER 30

"Give, and it will be given
to you."
Luke 6:38

Being a mother is a great honor and an awesome undertaking. It requires a great deal of giving—giving love, giving praise, giving encouragement, giving spankings, giving wisdom—giving it all! But we don't have to go it alone. On the days when we have nothing left to give, God does. He will supply all of our needs. He will give to us so that we can give to our families.

OCTOBER 31

So we say with confidence,
"The Lord is my helper;
I will not be afraid."
Hebrews 13:6

*I*don't know about you, but I sometimes feel afraid. Sure, I put on a good outward appearance, but on the inside I feel insecure. God did not give us a spirit of fear, but of love and power and a sound mind. We are up to any challenge. We can do all things through Him. We can be confident in Him today and every day.

NOVEMBER 1

"Then if my people who are called by my name
will humble themselves and pray and seek my face
and turn from their wicked ways,
I will hear from heaven and
will forgive their sins and restore their land."
2 Chronicles 7:14 NLT

*T*hank You, Lord, for America. Please direct and guide our leaders, and protect those men and women who protect us. Amen.

NOVEMBER 2

Our Father which art in heaven,
Hallowed be thy name.
Thy kingdom come. Thy will be done in earth,
as it is in heaven.
Give us this day our daily bread.
And forgive us our debts, as we forgive our debtors.
And lead us not into temptation, but deliver us from evil:
For thine is the kingdom, and the power,
and the glory, for ever. Amen.
Matthew 6:9–13 KJV

If you haven't taught your children the words to the Lord's Prayer, why not begin today?

NOVEMBER 3

"Your Father knows exactly what
you need even before you ask him!"
Matthew 6:8 NLT

Even when we can't pray what we want to pray, God knows our hearts. He knows what we need. If all we can do is say the name of Jesus, thankfully, that is enough. No matter how desperate you may be, God loves you. He wants to help you. He wants to help your children. Call on Him today.

NOVEMBER 4

Be joyful always; pray continually;
give thanks in all circumstances,
for this is God's will for you in Christ Jesus.
1 Thessalonians 5:16–18

One of the happiest people I've known was a man whose life had been filled with heartache. Still, he'd praise the Lord and share how wonderful Jesus had been to him. I want to be more like that. I want my children to be more like that, too. Let's go into Thanksgiving season with true gratefulness in our hearts.

NOVEMBER 5

Very early in the morning, while it was still dark,
Jesus got up, left the house and went off to a solitary place,
where he prayed.
Mark 1:35

You can pray all the time—continually—as it says in 1 Thessalonians, but you can also set a designated time for really intense, focused prayer. Do whatever works for you, but just do it. Make prayer a priority in your life today.

NOVEMBER 6

And he said: "I tell you the truth,
unless you change and become like little children,
you will never enter the kingdom of heaven."
Matthew 18:3

I've learned a lot about prayer from my children. They have taught me to pray with enthusiasm, thanksgiving, and expectation. As moms, we need to have that same thankful heart and expectation when we pray to our heavenly Father. Learn from your little ones. They truly know how to pray.

NOVEMBER 7

Pray continually.
1 Thessalonians 5:17

*E*ver since I read that Billy Graham said he prays without ceasing, I have endeavored to continually dialogue with God. At first, it seemed awkward. I struggled with it, wondering what to say. But after awhile, it became kind of second nature. I'd start praying without even realizing it. I'm certainly no Billy Graham, but I am enjoying this continual conversation with God. Go for it! Talk to God about everything. It's a wonderful way to live.

NOVEMBER 8

"Again, I tell you that if two of you
on earth agree about anything you ask for,
it will be done for you by my Father in heaven."
Matthew 18:19

According to this verse, if any two agree on something and ask the Father, it will be done. Well, I've got good news—we qualify as any! So, the next time you have an urgent request, grab your kids and ask them to agree with you. Your family's prayers avail much!

NOVEMBER 9

My help comes from the LORD,
the Maker of heaven and earth.
He will not let your foot slip—
he who watches over you will not slumber.
Psalm 121:2–3

God will answer your prayers, no matter what time of day. He is on call all the time!

Thank You, Lord, for always listening to my prayers. Amen.

November 10

Devote yourselves to prayer
with an alert mind and a thankful heart.
Colossians 4:2 NLT

*D*o you ever fall asleep during your prayer sessions? As moms (especially new moms), we get so few hours of sleep that once we're still for a few moments, we tend to fall asleep. Ask God to help you be alert during your prayer periods. He will help you. And even if you still fall asleep, God won't be offended. He will be waiting when you wake up.

November 11

Count yourself lucky, how happy you must be—
you get a fresh start, your slate's wiped clean.
Psalm 32:1 MSG

*I*sn't it nice that with God we always get to start over? No matter what we've done. No matter how disappointed we are in ourselves, God still loves us and forgives us. And the best part is that we get to wipe the slate clean! All we have to do is repent. Then we get to move forward with our heavenly Father.

NOVEMBER 12

O God, let me sing
a new song to you.
Psalm 144:9 MSG

The only way out of a prayer rut is to sing a new song. God is a good God. He is worthy of our praise. If you have trouble thinking of things to praise Him for during your prayer time, use the Bible to help. Quote scriptures. Get out of your rut and praise Him from the bottom of your heart.

NOVEMBER 13

Faith is the confidence that what we hope for
will actually happen.
Hebrews 11:1 NLT

Prayer works. It doesn't just work once in awhile. It doesn't just work when a minister prays for you. Prayer works all the time. There's only one requirement—have faith. You have to believe that the Lord is willing and able to meet your needs—no matter what they are. You have to know that He is all-powerful, all-knowing, and altogether merciful.

NOVEMBER 14

Do not be anxious about anything, but in everything,
by prayer and petition, with thanksgiving,
present your requests to God.
Philippians 4:6

My friend prays about absolutely everything. She prays about things that I wouldn't think to bring before God. But she is seeing great results. She has challenged me to pray more—even about little things—and I'm excited to see God's manifestation in my girls' lives..I challenge you to pray more, too. God wants to hear it all!

NOVEMBER 15

Now when Daniel learned that the decree had been published,
he went home to his upstairs room
where the windows opened toward Jerusalem.
Three times a day he got down on his knees
and prayed, giving thanks to his God,
just as he had done before.
Daniel 6:10

Lord, help me to slow down in order to hear from You. Amen.

November 16

*Then Jesus told his disciples a parable to show
them that they should always pray and not give up.*
Luke 18:1

Are you waiting for God to answer a very important prayer request? Are you getting weary in praying about this matter? Don't give up! Don't quit. Your answer, your ultimate victory, may be right around the corner. Keep praying because God is still listening and working on your behalf.

November 17

If we don't know how or what to pray,
it doesn't matter.
He does our praying in and for us,
making prayer out of our wordless sighs,
our aching groans.
Romans 8:26 MSG

I once read this beautiful statement: "God hears more than words. He listens to the heart." That means even if I can't communicate with words, God hears my heart cries. If you're hurting today and having trouble knowing what to pray, just cry out to God. He understands.

November 18

*"If you stand your ground, knocking
and waking all the neighbors,
he'll finally get up and get you whatever you need."*
Luke 11:8 MSG

Isn't it good to know that our prayers never inconvenience God? We can call on Him for help any time of day, for any reason at all. Let Him be your lifesaver today!

November 19

*"That's why I urge you to pray for absolutely everything,
ranging from small to large.
Include everything as you embrace this God-life,
and you'll get God's everything."*
Mark 11:24 MSG

Do you pray specifically or do you pray broad, general prayers? If you're praying general prayers, you're missing out. God wants us to pray specifically about small and large matters. He wants us to bring everything to Him. Praise God for the expected answers to your prayers and get ready for your miracles!

NOVEMBER 20

Then they brought him a demon-possessed man
who was blind and mute, and Jesus healed him,
so that he could both talk and see.
Matthew 12:22

Sometimes prayer is the best we can offer. Other times, we need to pray and act. In other words, don't use prayer as an excuse not to take action when you know you should do something. Follow the Holy Spirit's leading. Don't stop with praying. Go that extra mile and be a part of the solution.

NOVEMBER 21

When you ask, you do not receive,
because you ask with wrong motives.
James 4:3

Sometimes our prayers aren't answered because it's not in God's timing. Other times, they aren't answered because we haven't prayed in faith. Still other times, it's because we're praying with the wrong motivation. It's easy to fall into the wrong thinking which leads to the wrong kind of praying. If you're not seeing any answers to your prayers, check your motivation. That may be holding up your miracle.

November 22

It is good to praise the LORD and make music to your name,
O Most High,
to proclaim your love in the morning
and your faithfulness at night.
Psalm 92:1–2

Psalm 92 says that it's good to proclaim God's love in the morning. Spend those first few minutes each day praising the Lord. And whether you're a "wee hours of the morning" kind of gal or a "first thing in the morning" person, use that time to praise the Lord. Give God praise, and you'll have a much better day.

November 23

Is any one of you in trouble?
He should pray.
James 5:13

Is prayer your first instinct? This verse doesn't say to call your best friend and have her pray, or even to call your pastor. It says for you to pray. It's okay if we have others supporting us in prayer as long as we also pray. And if we teach our children to turn to prayer as their first line of defense, they'll forever be all right.

NOVEMBER 24

"When I fed them, they were satisfied;
when they were satisfied, they became proud;
then they forgot me."
Hosea 13:6

Like me, have you ever been guilty of the "run to God in bad times but ignore Him when things are good" syndrome? The scary crisis passes, and our prayers become fewer. We need God in the good times as much as in the bad times. Keep in touch with Him all the time. It's the only way to live.

NOVEMBER 25

In him and through faith in him
we may approach God
with freedom and confidence.
Ephesians 3:12

Do you know what really gets on my very last nerve? Those automated telephone systems. I'm so thankful that God doesn't have an automated answering system. ("Press 1 to praise. Press 2 to submit a prayer request. Press 3 to repent. Press 4 for wisdom. Press 0 if this is a real emergency.") Hallelujah, our heavenly Father is available 24/7! Call on Him today!

NOVEMBER 26

Do not be anxious about anything, but in everything,
by prayer and petition, with thanksgiving,
present your requests to God.
And the peace of God, which transcends all understanding,
will guard your hearts
and your minds in Christ Jesus.
Philippians 4:6–7

What kind of prayers are you praying? What kind of prayers are you teaching your children to pray? Begin praising the Lord for the victories that are on the way. Pray faith-filled prayers, and you'll begin to see results!

NOVEMBER 27

And my God will meet all your needs
according to his glorious riches in Christ Jesus.
Philippians 4:19

I am so thankful that God never tires of our requests. Like our kids do with us, we can bombard Him with requests—but He never gets sick of it. In fact, He wants us to bring all of our concerns to Him. He won't meet all our needs if we don't bring all of them to Him. Go ahead. Call on God right now!

NOVEMBER 28

Yes, you will lie down
and your sleep will be sweet.
Proverbs 3:24 NKJV

As moms, we want to make everything all right for our children. It's what we do. But as hard as we try, we can't fix everything. And worrying about the things we can't fix doesn't help, either. It just causes us to lose sleep and require wood putty to cover our dark circles! The next time you're up worrying, give it to God and then go to sleep.

NOVEMBER 29

"But when you pray, go into your room,
close the door and pray. . . .
Then your Father, who sees what
is done in secret, will reward you."
Matthew 6:6

We need to find time to pray every day. That may take some planning on your part. When my girls were toddlers, I was able to steal some time away with the Father in the sanctuary of our bathroom. Find something that works for you and stick to it. The Father is waiting. . . .

November 30

But Jesus Himself would often
slip away to the wilderness and pray.
Luke 5:16 NASB

*E*very time I have nothing left to give, Jesus reminds me that it's time to "retreat and replenish." By spending time on my knees and in His Word, I am refilled with God's love, strength, and joy. I give God all my worries, tiredness, and grouchiness, and He gives me all the good stuff. What a deal! Do yourself and your family a favor—retreat and replenish.

December 1

If you'll take a good, hard look at my pain,
If you'll quit neglecting me and go into action for me
By giving me a son,
I'll give him completely,
unreservedly to you.
I'll set him apart for a life of holy discipline.
1 Samuel 1:11 MSG

*T*hank You, Lord, for giving me children. I pray for those who are still trying to conceive or adopt. Please give them peace and patience as they wait for their miracle. Amen.

DECEMBER 2

Hannah did not go. She said to her husband,
"After the boy is weaned, I will take him
and present him before the LORD,
and he will live there always."
1 Samuel 1:22

Are you honoring God today? Have you given your children to God? After all, He gave them to you. Giving your kids to God is the best thing you could ever do for your children. Give them to God today and every day.

DECEMBER 3

Glory in his holy name;
let the hearts of those
who seek the LORD rejoice.
1 Chronicles 16:10

My daughters are in the tween stage—in between kids and teens. It's an exciting age, but a difficult one. Suddenly, everything I suggest is totally uncool. There are days when I feel totally useless and sorry for myself. But in God's presence I feel complete and useful once again. He builds me up, giving me the joy and strength I need to move forward.

DECEMBER 4

If I give all I possess to the poor
and surrender my body to the flames,
but have not love, I gain nothing.
1 Corinthians 13:3

Sometimes you give and give, and it never seems to be enough. We may get perturbed over our kids' ungrateful spirits and then give some more but in the wrong spirit. I wonder how God feels when He gives and gives, and then we want something different. No matter what, we should always keep a grateful heart.

DECEMBER 5

"If you, then, though you are evil,
know how to give good gifts to your children,
how much more will your Father in
heaven give good gifts to those who ask him!"
Matthew 7:11

Moms are natural-born givers. We simply love to bless our kids. But we don't have to have a lot of money to give good things to our children. The greatest gift my parents gave me was a love for Jesus. If we teach our children about Jesus, we've given them the greatest gift of all!

DECEMBER 6

Those who know your name will trust in you,
for you, LORD, have never forsaken
those who seek you.
Psalm 9:10

I struggle a bit when it comes to trusting God with my children. You see, trusting means giving God all of my worries and fears, and all of my dreams, concerning my kids. If you're having trouble trusting God with your children, get back in His Word. Read over all of the promises. You can trust Him with everything—even your children.

DECEMBER 7

He who gives to the poor
will lack nothing.
Proverbs 28:27

It's almost Christmas. We are in that gift-buying mode. It's fun! It's busy! It's tradition! But it's not an activity that everyone can afford to do. Why not "adopt" a needy family this holiday season? Get your children involved in shopping for the kids in that family or baking cookies for them. Give love this Christmas. It truly is the gift that keeps on giving.

DECEMBER 8

*"For God so loved the world that he gave
his one and only Son, that whoever
believes in him shall not perish
but have eternal life."*
John 3:16

*E*specially at this time when giving is so important, we need for our children to see us giving God our best. Our best praise, our best attention, our best love. After all, God gave us His very best when He sent Jesus more than two thousand years ago. He certainly deserves our best.

DECEMBER 9

*"So in everything, do to others what
you would have them do to you."*
Matthew 7:12

*W*ouldn't it be great if all of us lived every day just looking for any way to help others? I've been challenged to think of others' needs before my own. I hope you'll be challenged to do the same. Let's start giving of ourselves today.

DECEMBER 10

"As for God, his way is perfect;
the word of the LORD is flawless.
He is a shield for all who take refuge in him."
2 Samuel 22:31

We do the best we can as Christian moms. But our children will still make mistakes. They are no more perfect than we are. That's a scary thought, eh? There's only One who is perfect, and as long as we point our children toward Him, then we've done the very best that we can do.

DECEMBER 11

"It would be better for him if a millstone were hung
around his neck, and he were thrown into the sea,
than that he should offend one of these little ones."
Luke 17:2 NKJV

Do you know that everywhere we go, we are witnessing? At every moment, we are either glorifying God or portraying a poor reflection of Him. Our children are basing their view of Christianity on how we behave. So go forth and give a good witness. You have an attentive audience nearby.

DECEMBER 12

But Jesus said, "Let the little children
come to Me, and do not forbid them;
for of such is the kingdom of heaven."
Matthew 19:14 NKJV

*P*arents today are quite proactive. They have their unborn babies on the waiting lists for the top preschools in the area. They have college funds established before their children have ever spoken their first words. Let's be proactive about attending a church that will nurture and encourage our children's spiritual development. There's nothing more important.

DECEMBER 13

"For the LORD does not see as man sees;
for man looks at the outward appearance,
but the LORD looks at the heart."
1 Samuel 16:7 NKJV

*S*ometimes we need to get our hearts right in order to get our prayers right. If our heart motivation is wrong, our prayers will be useless. If you're not seeing results in your prayer life, ask the Holy Spirit to do a heart check on you. Prayers from a pure heart are more effective.

DECEMBER 14

As each one has received a gift,
minister it to one another.
1 Peter 4:10 NKJV

As moms, we need to give our children little tidbits of truth every day. Give them your knowledge and watch them grow. It's exciting!

DECEMBER 15

We must pay more careful attention,
therefore, to what we have heard,
so that we do not drift away.
Hebrews 2:1

If you get busy with your children and neglect your time with the Father, you won't stay; you'll drift away. Make time for God so that you will move forward with Him every day.

DECEMBER 16

In the same way,
the Spirit helps us in our weakness.
Romans 8:26

Lord, help me to help my children be strong in the face of peer pressure. Amen.

DECEMBER 17

Jesus Christ is the same yesterday,
today, and forever.
Hebrews 13:8 NLT

Jesus is the ultimate when it comes to consistency. Since we are commanded to be like Him, we have a right to ask God to help us in this area of consistency. The Holy Spirit will help us. It's not easy. It takes effort, but if you'll commit to being consistent in your parenting, your children will become consistently happier kids.

DECEMBER 18

My son, pay attention to what I say;
listen closely to my words.
Do not let them out of your sight,
keep them within your heart.
Proverbs 4:20–21

Lord, help me to retain the good stuff in Your Word and share it with others—especially my children. Amen.

DECEMBER 19

That you do not become sluggish,
but imitate those who through faith
and patience inherit the promises.
Hebrews 6:12 NKJV

It's so hard to have patience, isn't it? As mothers, we are doers. We don't wait for somebody else to act or take care of the situation. But what happens when the situation is out of our hands? That's where patience comes in. It gives us the strength to hold strong when our prayers aren't being answered immediately. Press on in patience.

DECEMBER 20

Do not throw away this confident trust in the Lord.
Remember the great reward it brings you!
Patient endurance is what you need now,
so that you will continue to do God's will.
Then you will receive all that he has promised.
Hebrews 10:35–36 NLT

No matter what you're facing today, God has given you a promise to handle it. Don't dwell on the problem. Meditate on the Master. He has made you more than a conqueror and has guaranteed your victory.

DECEMBER 21

"I will prevent pests from devouring your crops,
and the vines in your fields will not cast their fruit,"
says the LORD Almighty.
"Then all the nations will call you blessed,
for yours will be a delightful land,"
says the LORD Almighty."
Malachi 3:11–12

Heavenly Father, thank You for promising to provide for me. I trust in You. Amen.

DECEMBER 22

"Do not despise these small beginnings,
for the LORD rejoices to
see the work begin."
Zechariah 4:10 NLT

*S*ometimes, we get caught up in the parenting and forget how precious our kids are. We need to give them more credit because they are awesome creatures. We need to see them through our eyes of faith. Ask the Lord to help you see your children as He sees them. They are precious in His sight!

DECEMBER 23

Because of that experience, we have even greater
confidence in the message proclaimed by the prophets.
You must pay close attention to what they wrote,
for their words are like a lamp shining in a dark place—
until the Day dawns, and
Christ the Morning Star shines in your hearts.
2 Peter 1:19 NLT

*J*esus is known as the Light of the World. And His Word sheds light on every situation and drives out the darkness of confusion. C'mon, step into the light.

December 24

*"What stories you can tell your children
and grandchildren about the incredible
things I am doing."*
Exodus 10:2 TLB

*I*t's my most favorite night of the year. It's not because of the yummy sweets or the gifts, but because our family is all together. After everything settles down, my father always reads the Christmas story. Whatever your traditions, I hope you'll give your children the true meaning of Christmas this year. Jesus is the reason for the season.

December 25

*Then Peter came to Jesus and asked,
"Lord, how many times shall I forgive
my brother when he sins against me?
Up to seven times?" Jesus answered,
"I tell you, not seven times,
but seventy-seven times."*
Matthew 18:21–22

*C*hristmas is a time when family members get together. If you've been harboring unforgiveness against someone in your family, give the gift of forgiveness this year. You'll receive gifts in return—freedom, love, joy, and more! And you'll have a merry Christmas!

DECEMBER 26

"I am the vine; you are the branches.
If a man remains in me and I in him,
he will bear much fruit."
John 15:5

We can celebrate Christmas all year because Jesus lives inside us! We can look forward to each day just to see what He has in store for us. If you know someone who is depressed this time of year, why not share Jesus with that person? Give the gift of Jesus—the gift who truly keeps on giving.

DECEMBER 27

But the fruit of the Spirit is love, joy, peace,
patience, kindness, goodness, faithfulness,
gentleness and self-control.
Galatians 5:22–23

Every day, we have opportunities to share joy or share ugliness. Choose joy. Our joyful spirits will win others for Jesus. They'll want whatever it is we've got! So go forth and be joyful today!

DECEMBER 28

I will be glad and rejoice in you;
I will sing praise to your name,
O Most High.
Psalm 9:2

Instead of feeling guilty or regretful over past mistakes, take time to think on the good things that God did through you and in you and for you this year. Think on all of the miracles He performed on behalf of your family. Let God know that you appreciate Him. That's the way to close one year and begin another—praising God!

DECEMBER 29

I can do everything through
him who gives me strength.
Philippians 4:13

Lord, I need Your help today. Help me to accomplish _____ that I've been putting off for too long. I can't do it alone, but I know You will help me. Amen.

DECEMBER 30

"Submit to God and
be at peace with him."
Job 22:21

*P*eace is very popular during the holidays, but as Christians we can enjoy peace throughout the year. If we let God in and give Him total control of our lives, we are guaranteed peace. Jesus wasn't just called "the Prince of Peace," He is the Prince of Peace. Turn to Him today. Give peace priority in your life.

DECEMBER 31

But the fruit of the Spirit is love,
joy, peace, patience, kindness, goodness, faithfulness,
gentleness and self-control.
Galatians 5:22–23

*L*et me tell you what's even better than giving a fruit basket or a fruitcake—giving the fruit of the Spirit. Our children need to see us walking in those qualities of love, joy, peace, patience, kindness, goodness, faithfulness, gentleness, and self-control. And we don't have to just give them during the holidays—we can radiate those qualities year round!

NOTES

NOTES

THE WAY TO JESUS CHRIST IS SIMPLE:

1. ADMIT THAT YOU ARE A SINNER.

For all have sinned, and come short
of the glory of God.
ROMANS 3:23

2. BELIEVE THAT JESUS IS GOD THE SON WHO PAID THE WAGES OF YOUR SIN.

For the wages of sin is death [eternal separation
from God]; but the gift of God is eternal life
through Jesus Christ our Lord.
ROMANS 6:23

3. CALL UPON GOD.

If thou shalt confess with thy mouth the Lord Jesus,
and shalt believe in thine heart that God hath raised him
from the dead, thou shalt be saved.
ROMANS 10:9

SALVATION IS A VERY PERSONAL THING
BETWEEN YOU AND GOD.
THE DECISION IS YOURS ALONE.